`THE

Lunch Box

COOKBOOK

MARTY KLINZMAN

Photography by Peter Brooks and Malcolm Dare

NEW
HOLLAND

First published in the UK in 1993 by
New Holland (Publishers) Ltd
37 Connaught Street, London W2 2AZ

ISBN 1 85368 268 3 (hbk)
ISBN 1 85368 257 8 (pbk)

Designer: Janice Evans
Assistant designer: Lellyn Creamer
Reproduction by Fotoplate (Pty) Ltd
Printed and bound in Singapore by Tien Wah Press (Pte) Ltd

Photographers' Acknowledgments
Peter Brooks: pages 4, 5, 6, 7, 13, 19, 21, 22, 27, 30, 33, 34, 43, 47,
50, 54, 57, 60, 63, 64 (top right)
Copyright © 1993 New Holland (Publishers) Ltd

Malcolm Dare: pages 1, 2, 3, 9, 11, 15, 17, 20, 23, 24, 29, 31, 37, 38,
41, 45, 49, 52, 59, 64 (bottom left), front and back covers
Copyright © 1993 New Holland (Publishers) Ltd

CONTENTS

INTRODUCTION

This book is intended to help you dispel the lunch-box blues every packed-lunch eater gets when he or she hopefully opens box, bag or briefcase only to find soggy sandwiches hiding beneath limp lettuce. Brighten up packed lunches with the exciting ideas in this book. You won't find recipes for five-course meals between these pages, but you will find plenty of ideas to help you create appetising, healthy fare for the hungry schoolchild, office executive, secretary or slimmer; even recipes to make and take along on a picnic. There are suggestions for sandwich fillings, healthy treats to satisfy a sweet tooth and a large selection of goodies to make, bake, pack and send to children at boarding school or sons and daughters away at college. You will find information on containers and how to pack them and on how to freeze and serve a portable feast.

Use a bit of imagination when you pack the lunch box and make lunch something to look forward to. Include hot foods – soups, chilli, stews – during winter months, packed in wide-mouthed thermos flasks. Add extras like cheese, devilled eggs, salads, relishes, finger foods or something sweet. All the recipes are in these pages. Bon appetit!

THE PORTABLE FEAST

Dedicated lunch-carriers know that a portable feast makes good sense: the packed lunch saves time and money during a busy day. You don't have to go out in search of expensive take-aways; you can cater for individual likes and dislikes and allow for food allergies. You can keep a check on calories by including foods high in nutritional value but low in fats and carbohydrates and you can be in control of your family's eating habits.

A packed lunch should supply about one-third of the nutrients required for the day. A good, nutritious lunch increases productivity and endurance, so encourage healthy eating by making the lunch box as attractive and appealing as possible. The packed lunch must be easy to carry and easy to eat. A well-planned meal need take up only a small space in school bag, handbag or briefcase but, if the lunch is quite substantial or a thermos of hot or cold food is included, a special container or bag may be needed. Adults may find it convenient to keep a can opener, small salt and pepper shakers and a knife and fork at the office. Students prefer foods that are easy to handle and consume, such as sandwiches, fresh fruit, hard-boiled eggs and small cakes and biscuits, while teachers will appreciate it if their students' lunches don't contain messy items.

Keeping packed lunches in good condition is important for fresh flavour and healthy eating. Make sure utensils and work surfaces where food is prepared are clean and keep perishable foods chilled or frozen until the lunches are packed. Try adding a small frozen can or box of fruit juice, a frozen carton of yoghurt or a small commercial cold pack to the lunch box to keep foods cool during the morning. Remind children not to stash sandwiches and other foods on top of the classroom radiator or on a hot window sill. Read 'For Safety's Sake' (page 44) for more ideas on serving safe foods.

MENU PLANNING

Good nutrition depends on good eating habits and these do not just happen. Menus that are carefully planned will foster good eating habits in youngsters and reinforce them in the adults in your family.

You can save time, and money too, by planning meals for a week or longer. Once the menus are planned it is easy to make shopping lists and plan for foods that can be prepared in advance. You will feel confident that your family will be well fed without the everyday problem of deciding what to make for lunch.

Attractive, delicious and nutritious – that is a good description of a well-planned lunch. The way food looks will be noticed first. If colours and shapes of food contrast attractively, the meal will look good enough to eat. Taste, of course, is an equally important factor: flavours and textures should complement each other. Here are some useful tips that will help you to plan interesting and appetising lunches:

☆ Serve a crisp food with a soft one.
☆ Accent bland flavours with something spicy or tart.
☆ Season carefully to bring out the best flavours, but do not over season.
☆ Something hot packed with something cold makes a good combination.
☆ Plan puddings that really go with the meal – a light dessert will complement a heavy meal, while a rich dessert will be the perfect end to a light meal.
☆ Plan snacks as part of the day's requirements of nutrients and avoid having too many that are sugary or starchy.

Meal planning is not as difficult as people think it is and you do not have to be a dietitian to create a balanced menu. Foods can be divided into five basic groups and with wise selections from each group, you can provide your family with a balanced diet. Select the recommended amounts of foods from the following categories:

Milk and dairy products

Every member of your family needs some milk. Count on these quantities each day: children and teenagers need 500–750 ml (17–25 fl oz), adults 300–400 ml (10–14 fl oz) per day. Provide milk to drink, or use it in cooking. Other dairy foods that count towards the total intake are cheese, yoghurt and ice-cream.

Meat, fish, poultry, cheese, nuts and pulses

The foods in this group are good sources of protein and also contain iron and B vitamins. Members of your family need two or more servings each day. Vary the protein foods eaten daily to include fish, poultry, cheese or eggs, and remember that baked beans, nuts and peanut butter also count towards a serving.

Breads, cereals and grains

The foods in this group, which include pasta and rice, contain carbohydrates for energy as well as vitamins, minerals, fibre and some proteins. An average of three servings a day will supply the necessary nutrients. Baked foods such as biscuits and cakes also count towards a serving. Sugar is included here but should be served in limited amounts. If a packed lunch consists of sandwiches, try to avoid serving bread at breakfast and supper.

Fruits and vegetables

These foods are rich in vitamins and minerals. The variety that is available makes it easy to provide three or more servings each day. Serve a citrus fruit or other fruit rich in vitamin C and a dark green or deep yellow vegetable (for vitamin A) each day. Snacks can provide a serving – add crisp vegetable sticks or fresh fruit to the lunch box.

Fats and oils

Foods in this group help provide energy. Butter and margarine also contain vitamins A and D. Many foods contain fat that we cannot see, so butter spread on bread and an oil-based salad dressing will provide the necessary daily requirements.

DOVETAIL AND DOUBLE UP

Learn to dovetail your food preparation. If you heat up the oven for a roast, bake a loaf of bread at the same time and keep it in the freezer. Plan leftovers to supply fillings for sandwiches or a main part of the packed lunch. Double recipes for biscuits and other baked goods, store them in the freezer and you will have snacks for months to come.

*Good eating starts with
a variety of good foods*

THE KITCHEN CUPBOARD

Organising the kitchen for lunch-making will help save time. Set aside a little space for keeping items needed for the lunch box and for its preparation. Keep a supply of plastic containers with lids: use small ones for puddings, fruits and soft foods; square or rectangular ones hold sandwiches or main courses. Plastic bags in a variety of sizes and plastic cling-film are useful for packaging sandwiches, vegetables or snacks. Thermos flasks hold hot or cold foods and come in a variety of sizes, so you may wish to keep one or two of these. It is a good idea to put a name on lunch containers, especially for children who may forget to bring them home. Make a space in your kitchen cupboard for salt, pepper, butter or margarine, mustard, tomato ketchup and a supply of paper napkins to tuck into the lunch box. Sturdy plastic cutlery will provide eating utensils and it won't matter if they are lost or left behind.

Organise the storage area near a good work surface so stacks of sandwiches can be made or several lunches packed at once.

A MATTER OF CONVENIENCE
(The shop-and-serve lunch)

Supermarket shelves and freezers hold an array of pre-cooked, pre-packaged foods that are good lunch additions. You can purchase individual meat pies, pasties and savouries to pack with a salad or fruit for a satisfying meal. Small cans of corned beef, meat or fish spread, pâtés and cheese spreads will fit easily into the lunch container but be sure to include a tin opener!

Cooked meats from the delicatessen are pre-sliced and make good sandwich fillings. Most of them freeze well, so sandwiches can be made in advance when meat and bread are freshest. Cheeses are often packaged in convenient individual servings and make good snacks to add to the lunch box. Small cans of vegetables, baked beans and salads can also be added for a hearty packed lunch. Even desserts and sweet snacks are available in one-serving portions. Chocolate or vanilla puddings, individual trifles, fruit pies, yoghurts and dried fruit bars qualify as lunch-time favourites and sweet biscuits such as muesli cookies do contain more than just sugar.

You will find the prices slightly higher than for home-made foods but keep prepared foods in mind and use them when time is short – as a matter of convenience.

NOTE: ✳ This symbol indicates that the recipe freezes well.

SCHOOL BREAK

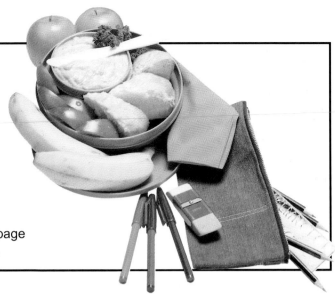

Hungry children need a filling and nutritious lunch after a morning session in the classroom. They need fuel to fire their bodies and minds for afternoon lessons and extra-mural activities too, so packing a healthy, appetising and satisfying lunch is an important part of a busy mum's morning. Lunch bags are not, of course, legally bound to contain sandwiches but the sandwich is the traditional, versatile and convenient holder for protein-rich foods. Sandwiches are easy to make (see 'The Great Sandwich', page 11), simple to eat and a favourite food with the younger set.

Whatever you decide to pack in the lunch box, follow this useful quick guide to good nutrition and include:

A protein-rich food Sandwich, soup, fried chicken or fish, casserole, meat pie or cheese.

A fruit or vegetable Fresh vegetable pieces or salad, whole fresh fruit or canned fruit.

Something extra A sweet treat that could be called dessert but that is not too sugar-laden.

Something for a snack A healthy, crunchy food.

Beverage If no provisions are made at the school, pack fruit or vegetable juice.

The choice of container in which to carry lunch to school will depend on what is 'in' at the moment. It may be quite acceptable to your child and his peers to place the lunch suitably wrapped or packed in his school bag, or if that is 'out', perhaps the bright shiny lunch box is 'in'. You can provide rigid plastic containers with tightly fitting lids to protect delicate items and thermos flasks are useful for keeping hot meals hot and cold meals well chilled.

A varied packed lunch may not be as important to the schoolchild as it is to an adult, so it might be a good idea to decide on a limited selection of favourites that will meet with the approval of the younger members of your family. The school lunch may not be the best place to introduce new foods and flavours to a child – it is likely that such foods will be swapped or end up in the rubbish bin.

The menus in the box on this page provide suggestions for school lunches.

SCHOOL BREAK MENUS

Chilli con carne (page 23)
Yoghurt dill dip (page 10)
* with crisp vegetables*
Crispy marshmallow squares
* (page 10)*

Crisp fried chicken
Cheese spread (page 8)
* with Wholemeal banana*
* bread (page 17)*
Orange

Stacked salad (page 8) with Green
* goddess dip (page 10)*
Ham and cheese muffin (page 7)
Fresh fruit
Peanuts and popcorn (page 35)

Peanut butter filling (page 12)
* on Batter oat bread (page 18)*
Stuffed celery sticks (page 8)
Orange and banana fruit salad
* (page 42)*

Egg in pitta (page 8)
Crisp vegetable pieces
* with Bacon dip (page 10)*
Fresh fruit
Oat and banana biscuit (page 61)

Bean and bacon spread (page 8)
* with Cheesy scones (page 58)*
Tomato wedges
Fresh fruit
Peanut balls (page 10)

Tomato soup
Liver-sausage spread (page 8) on
* Wholemeal bread (page 18)*
Delightfully devilled eggs (page 8)
Bunch of grapes

Tuna salad sandwich (page 14)
Pickles or olives
Vegetable dip (page 8)
* with crisp vegetable pieces*
Peanut butter granola bars
* (page 10)*

Pizza (page 23)
Pickles, radishes and celery sticks
* with Onion dip (page 10)*
Fresh pineapple chunks

Macaroni Bolognese (page 26)
Crunchy vegetables with
* Cucumber dip (page 10)*
Chocolate-topped crunchy bars
* (page 10)*

HAM AND CHEESE MUFFINS ❄

300 g (11 oz) plain flour
60 ml (4 tbsp) caster sugar
15 ml (1 tbsp) baking powder
60 g (2 oz) Cheddar cheese, grated
60 g (2 oz) cooked ham, finely
** chopped**
1 egg, beaten
200 ml (7 fl oz) milk
75 ml (5 tbsp) oil

Sift flour, sugar and baking powder into a large bowl. Add cheese and ham and mix in. Combine egg, milk and oil and add all at once to flour mixture. Stir until just moistened (batter will still be lumpy). Fill greased muffin tins two thirds full and bake at 200 °C (400 °F, gas 6) for 20–25 minutes. These muffins can be individually wrapped in clingfilm and frozen. They will thaw quickly in the lunch box.
MAKES 12 MUFFINS.

EGG IN PITTA

3 large, hard-boiled eggs, chopped
1 stick celery, chopped
30 ml (2 tbsp) mayonnaise
5 ml (1 tsp) prepared mild mustard
a little salt and pepper
4 Pitta breads (page 18)
8 slices processed cheese

Mix eggs, celery, mayonnaise and mustard and season with salt and pepper. Open the pittas, line each with 2 slices of cheese, then spoon in a quarter of the egg filling. Close the pittas and wrap well.
SERVES 4.

STACKED SALAD

1 small tomato, sliced
1 slice cooked ham, cut into quarters
1 hard-boiled egg, cut into wedges
1 slice cheese, cut into quarters
a few bean sprouts
30 ml (2 tbsp) Green goddess dip (page 10)

In a container, layer 2 slices of tomato, 2 quarters of ham, 2 egg wedges and 2 cheese quarters. Repeat layers and top with remaining tomato. Sprinkle with bean sprouts, cover and seal container. Chill well. Pack Green goddess dip separately to add just before eating.
SERVES 1.

STUFFED CELERY STICKS

These are healthy, crisp snacks. Cut fresh celery sticks into 10 cm (4 inch) lengths, then chill and stuff with any of the following combinations:

Nutty blue cheese Combine 250 ml (8 fl oz) curd cheese with 75 ml (5 tbsp) crumbled blue cheese and 60 ml (4 tbsp) chopped walnuts or pecan nuts. Stir in 2.5 ml (½ tsp) Worcestershire sauce.
Spicy cheese Combine 250 ml (8 fl oz) curd cheese with 1 finely chopped spring onion, 5 ml (1 tsp) chilli powder and 2.5 ml (½ tsp) garlic salt.
Lemon cheese Combine 250 ml (8 fl oz) curd cheese with 60 ml (4 tbsp) chopped celery leaves, grated rind of 1 lemon, 15 ml (1 tbsp) lemon juice and 2.5 ml (½ tsp) salt.
Fruity cheese Combine 250 ml (8 fl oz) curd cheese with 30 ml (2 tbsp) mayonnaise, 45 ml (3 tbsp) finely grated carrot, 30 ml (2 tbsp) raisins and 45 ml (3 tbsp) well-drained crushed pineapple.

DELIGHTFULLY DEVILLED EGGS

Devilled eggs make a nutritious savoury snack. To make devilled eggs for packing, cut hard-boiled eggs in half, remove yolks, mash, and mix with other desired ingredients. Fill egg halves and press back together to form a 'whole' egg. Wrap in clingfilm and chill before packing in the lunch box. Mash the yolks of 4 hard-boiled eggs with any of the following:

☆ 30 ml (2 tbsp) mayonnaise, salt and pepper to taste, a pinch of dry mustard and 30 ml (2 tbsp) finely grated cheese of your choice
☆ 30 ml (2 tbsp) mayonnaise, 15 ml (1 tbsp) pickle, salt and pepper to taste
☆ 30 ml (2 tbsp) curd cheese, 10 ml (2 tsp) chopped chives, salt and pepper to taste
☆ 30 ml (2 tbsp) mayonnaise, 15 ml (1 tbsp) white vinegar, 2.5 ml (½ tsp) curry powder
☆ 15 ml (1 tbsp) French dressing, 30 ml (2 tbsp) finely crumbled blue cheese, pepper to taste
☆ 15 ml (1 tbsp) soured cream, 5 ml (1 tsp) lemon juice, 15 ml (1 tbsp) chutney
☆ 30 ml (2 tbsp) mayonnaise, a little dry mustard, 15–30 ml (1–2 tbsp) finely chopped ham or bacon, pepper to taste

SPREADS AND DIPS

A meat or cheese spread makes a good snack with savoury biscuits or fingers of wholemeal bread. Don't forget to pack a plastic knife for spreading. Dips made of cream cheese, cottage cheese or natural yoghurt are great with crisp vegetables or fruit, and are filled with nutrients too.

Experiment by adding new flavours to the lunch box with the following recipes, which makes perfect snacks:

BEAN AND BACON SPREAD

100 g (3½ oz) baked beans, drained
90 ml (6 tbsp) curd cheese
3 rashers bacon, crisply fried and chopped
salt and pepper to taste

Place beans and cheese in a blender or food processor and blend until smooth, or mash well with a fork. Fold in bacon and season to taste with salt and pepper. Store in the refrigerator until ready to pack in the lunch box. Spread on savoury biscuits or wholemeal bread.
SERVES 2.

CHEESY SPREAD

90 ml (6 tbsp) cream cheese
60 g (2 oz) Cheddar cheese, finely grated
2.5 ml (½ tsp) Worcestershire sauce
few drops Tabasco
2.5 ml (½ tsp) lemon juice
30 ml (2 tbsp) chopped nuts

Mix cream cheese, Cheddar cheese, Worcestershire sauce, Tabasco and lemon juice. Pack into two containers, sprinkle chopped nuts over, cover and chill until ready to pack.
SERVES 2.

LIVER-SAUSAGE SPREAD

125 g (4 oz) liver sausage
30 ml (2 tbsp) single or soured cream
15 ml (1 tbsp) sunflower or sesame seeds

Combine all ingredients, mixing well. Pack into two small containers and store in the refrigerator until ready to pack in the lunch box with savoury biscuits or fresh wholemeal bread.
SERVES 2.

THE GREAT FROMAGE FRAIS DIP

You can make two or three individual dips from one carton of fromage frais. These dips keep well for over a week in the refrigerator, so make up a couple for easy, tasty snacks.

VEGETABLE DIP

125 ml (4 fl oz) fromage frais
30 g (1 oz) cucumber, peeled, chopped and seeded
15 ml (1 tbsp) pickle, finely chopped
5 ml (1 tsp) chopped chives
30 ml (2 tbsp) grated carrot
salt to taste
a little single cream

Mix fromage frais with cucumber, pickle, chives and grated carrot. Add salt to taste and a little cream to make a dipping consistency. Serve with cherry tomatoes or courgette wedges.
SERVES 2.

Clockwise from left: Pineapple dip, Green goddess dip and Vegetable dip

PINEAPPLE DIP

125 ml (4 fl oz) fromage frais
30 ml (2 tbsp) drained crushed
    pineapple
15 ml (1 tbsp) soured cream
2.5 ml (½ tsp) seasoning salt
2.5 ml (½ tsp) toasted sesame seeds

Mix fromage frais with pineapple, soured cream, seasoning salt and sesame seeds. Chill until needed. Serve with savoury biscuits or fresh vegetable slices.
SERVES 2.

BACON DIP

125 ml (4 fl oz) fromage frais
30 ml (2 tbsp) finely chopped blue
    cheese
5 ml (1 tsp) lemon juice
2 rashers bacon, cooked and crumbled
3 stuffed olives, chopped

Mix fromage frais with blue cheese, lemon juice, bacon and olives. Chill until needed. Delicious with celery sticks.
SERVES 2.

GREEN GODDESS DIP

60 ml (4 tbsp) fromage frais
5 ml (1 tsp) anchovy paste
2.5 ml (½ tsp) chopped fresh parsley
few drops Worcestershire sauce
good pinch dry mustard
few garlic flakes
5 ml (1 tsp) chopped chives
125 ml (4 fl oz) natural yoghurt

Place all ingredients except yoghurt in a blender and process until smooth. Stir in yoghurt and chill. Serve with green pepper strips or whole mushrooms.
SERVES 3.

QUICKIE DIPS

Banana dip Blend ½ banana with about 30 ml (2 tbsp) mayonnaise.
SERVES 1.
Peanut butter dip Whip 30 ml (2 tbsp) smooth peanut butter with 30 ml (2 tbsp) mayonnaise and a few drops milk. Serve with celery.
SERVES 1.
Lemon and honey dip Stir 5 ml (1 tsp) lemon juice and 5 ml (1 tsp) clear honey into 30 ml (2 tbsp) mayonnaise. Serve with apple wedges.
SERVES 1.

Cucumber dip Blend a 5 cm (2 inch) cucumber piece, peeled and seeded, with 90 ml (6 tbsp) natural yoghurt and a little salt in an electric blender.
SERVES 2.
Cashew dip Grind 60 g (2 oz) cashew nuts in a blender, add 15 ml (1 tbsp) oil and ½ ripe banana.
SERVES 1–2.

YOGHURT MIXERS

These dips are good with vegetable sticks or fruit, or as dressings for salads.

ONION DIP

250 ml (8 fl oz) natural yoghurt
30 ml (2 tbsp) white onion soup powder

Mix yoghurt and soup powder and leave overnight in the refrigerator. Serve with savoury biscuits or vegetable pieces.
SERVES 4.

YOGHURT DILL DIP

125 ml (4 fl oz) natural yoghurt
15 ml (1 tbsp) mayonnaise
2.5 ml (½ tsp) dried dill
10 ml (2 tsp) lemon juice
pinch dry mustard
pinch salt

Mix all ingredients together well and chill until ready to pack. Tomato wedges and cauliflower florets make good dippers.
SERVES 2.

CHOCOLATE-TOPPED CRUNCHY BARS ❊

125 g (4 oz) butter or margarine
60 ml (4 tbsp) clear honey
60 ml (4 tbsp) soft brown sugar
350 g (12 oz) rolled oats
2.5 ml (½ tsp) ground cinnamon
75 g (2½ oz) sultanas
100 g (3½ oz) milk chocolate, melted

In a large saucepan, melt butter or margarine. Add honey and sugar and stir to just mix. Add rolled oats, cinnamon and sultanas. Mix well. Press into a greased baking tin and bake at 200°C (400°F, gas 6) for about 10 minutes. Place on a wire rack to cool. Drizzle melted chocolate over mixture while still warm and cut into squares. Cool completely in the tin, then transfer to a container with a tightly fitting lid.
MAKES ABOUT 30 SQUARES.

PEANUT BALLS

90 g (3 oz) powdered milk
250 g (8 oz) smooth peanut butter
250 g (8 oz) clear honey
90 g (3 oz) sesame seeds
60 ml (4 tbsp) wheatgerm
1 egg white, lightly beaten
150 g (5 oz) peanuts, finely chopped

In a large bowl combine powdered milk, peanut butter, honey, sesame seeds and wheatgerm. Mix well and knead with hands until a smooth dough is formed. Cut into 36 pieces and roll each into a ball. Dip balls in beaten egg white, then in chopped peanuts. Allow to dry at room temperature, then store in a container with a tightly fitting lid.
MAKES 36 BALLS.

CRISPY MARSHMALLOW SQUARES ❊

125 g (4 oz) rice crispies
60 g (2 oz) butter
35 marshmallows
100 g (3½ oz) plain chocolate, coarsely
    grated (optional)
60 g (2 oz) pecan nuts, coarsely
    chopped

Place cereal in a large mixing bowl. In a large saucepan, melt the butter, then add marshmallows and heat, stirring, until the marshmallows have melted and the mixture is well blended. Pour over cereal. Add chocolate and nuts and mix to coat cereal well. Gently press mixture into a greased baking tin and allow to cool. When cool, cut into squares. These squares can be wrapped individually and frozen.
MAKES ABOUT 24 SQUARES.

PEANUT BUTTER GRANOLA BARS ❊

155 g (5 oz) golden syrup
few drops vanilla essence
185 g (6 oz) smooth peanut butter
250 g (9 oz) crunchy granola cereal
90 g (3 oz) raisins

Bring golden syrup and vanilla essence to the boil. Remove from heat, add peanut butter and stir until smooth. Stir in granola and raisins. Quickly spread mixture in a greased 23 cm (9 inch) square baking pan. Cool for 1 hour, cut into bars and store in a container with a tightly fitting lid, or wrap securely in clingfilm and freeze.
MAKES ABOUT 20 BARS.

THE GREAT SANDWICH

Medieval Scandinavian records prove that the sandwich is not a modern creation – meals were served between slices of bread even then. The name 'sandwich' is attributed to the fourth Earl of Sandwich, an avid gambler who refused to leave the tables even to eat. A clever chef thought of a way of serving him at the gambling table by using slices of bread as edible holders for roast meats.

In modern language, the sandwich refers to anything served on, or between, slices of bread. It is a versatile, convenient, neatly packaged meal-in-itself and a perfect main course for the packed lunch.

In this chapter you will find over 100 ideas for meat, cheese, fish, poultry and vegetarian fillings.

HINTS FOR SANDWICH MAKING

The perfect sandwich starts with fresh bread, so be sure to use only bread that is at its best.

☆ Make a whole batch of sandwiches quickly using assembly-line techniques. Line the slices of bread up in rows, two-by-two. Butter and fill sandwiches in one operation. Wrap well and freeze if desired.

☆ A serrated bread knife is useful for slicing fresh loaves without tearing the edges of slices. You may find that some breads will be easier to slice if turned on their sides. If you have an electric knife, use it to obtain neat slices of bread quickly without squashing the loaf.

☆ For easy spreading without tearing the bread, first soften the butter or margarine. Alternatively, freeze sliced bread, then butter while still frozen.

☆ Spread butter or margarine all the way to the edges of the crusts in an even layer. This will help to prevent moisture from the filling mixture from soaking into the bread. Don't trim off crusts as they keep sandwich edges from drying out.

☆ For assembly-line sandwiches, allow 16–20 slices of bread from a 500 g (18 oz) loaf. You will use about 500 g (18 oz) butter or margarine for every 3–4 of these loaves. Plan on using 75–90 ml (5–6 tbsp) filling for each sandwich. If the sandwiches are for hearty eaters, you may wish to allow up to 125 ml (4 fl oz) filling, but be sure that the filling is not too moist as it will leak.

☆ Have all materials ready when making sandwiches by the batch. You will need plastic sandwich bags with ties, clingfilm (freezer-proof if going into the freezer), plastic boxes with snug lids and labelling materials.

☆ Remember that the freezer will keep bread fresh longer, but bread that has been frozen will dry out quickly once it has thawed, so make sure that sandwiches are wrapped securely to keep freshness and flavour in.

☆ For variety, take advantage of the different flavours and shapes of breads, rolls and buns that are available.

☆ Children find it easier to eat sandwiches cut into four small wedges or squares than to wrestle with a whole sandwich.

☆ Put a little fun in the lunch box by using two kinds of bread for a sandwich. Try wholemeal and white, white and rye, or even granary and banana breads. Select slices that are the same size to ensure that the edges will fit together neatly.

☆ Pack lettuce, cucumber slices or tomato slices separately, otherwise they will make the sandwich soggy. Pack them securely in plastic sandwich bags, then at lunch time they can be added to the sandwich.

☆ When making sandwiches from leftover cooked meats, remember that it is easier to eat a sandwich containing three or four thin slices rather than one thick slice of meat.

☆ To make a change from lettuce, try adding a little watercress, spinach leaves, a little shredded cabbage, bean or other sprouts or sliced radishes to sandwiches. Pack these ingredients separately, then add at lunch time.

☆ A frozen sandwich packed in the lunch box will thaw by lunch time and be fresh and cool. A word of caution: sandwiches that contain large amounts of mayonnaise or fish paste will be safe until midday or longer only if kept in a cool place. See pages 54–56 for more hints on freezing sandwiches.

FILLING IDEAS

Even the most patient sandwich-eater will eventually tire of the same spread or filling placed between two slices of ordinary bread! That doesn't mean you have to abandon peanut butter or egg salad. It really is easy to add a little excitement to the familiar standby sandwich fillings, if you think ahead and plan new flavours to pack. These ideas should get you started:

CHEESE FILLINGS

With the variety of cheese on the market, it may be possible to pack a different cheese sandwich every day for a month. Smooth cream cheese, chunky cottage cheese and our good friends Cheddar and processed cheese can form the base for a great number of cheese sandwiches.

Try cottage cheese with:
☆ raisins and chopped nuts, such as pecans or walnuts, on fruit bread
☆ fried, crumbled bacon and drained crushed pineapple, on wholemeal bread
☆ diced cold meats, chopped pickles and chopped chives
☆ marmalade, jam or honey on fruit or nut breads
☆ finely chopped olives, toasted sesame seeds, salt and pepper, on a bagel
☆ finely chopped cooked chicken, finely chopped onion and salt and pepper
☆ crumbled blue cheese and a dash of Worcestershire sauce
☆ thin slices of cucumber, fresh parsley, onion, salt and lettuce
☆ apple slices brushed with lemon juice and a sprinkling of ground cinnamon, on fruit or nut bread
☆ chopped green olives and chopped pecan nuts
☆ sliced avocado brushed with lemon juice and sprinkled with sunflower seeds and bean or other sprouts

Try grated cheese, thin cheese slices or flavoured cheese spread with:
☆ tomato slices, lettuce and bean or other sprouts
☆ sliced apple, brushed with lemon juice
☆ thin cucumber slices and a few caraway seeds
☆ meat slices, lettuce and tomato

EGG FILLINGS

Egg salad sandwiches have long been a favourite of the lunch-box brigade. This basic recipe, which can be doubled if necessary, can be made in advance and refrigerated for 2–3 days, so make it up, then add any of the extras given below as desired.

BASIC EGG SALAD

2 hard-boiled eggs, chopped
1 small stick celery, finely chopped
15–20 ml (3–4 tsp) mayonnaise or salad cream
pinch dry mustard
salt and pepper to taste

In a small bowl, mash eggs until almost smooth. Add remaining ingredients and mix well. Keep refrigerated.
MAKES ENOUGH FOR 2–3 SANDWICHES.

For new egg salad ideas, add one or more of the following:
☆ 15 ml (1 tbsp) pickle
☆ 5 ml (1 tsp) prepared horseradish
☆ 2 rashers bacon, fried and crumbled

☆ 60 g (2 oz) ham, finely chopped
☆ 3–4 mushrooms, finely chopped
☆ sunflower or toasted sesame seeds
☆ finely chopped green pepper to taste
☆ bean or other sprouts
☆ 60 ml (4 tbsp) finely grated carrot
☆ 15 ml (1 tbsp) chopped fresh parsley
☆ 15 ml (1 tbsp) chopped spring onion
☆ curry powder to taste and 10 ml (2 tsp) chutney
☆ pinch dried tarragon, basil or sage
☆ 15 ml (1 tbsp) tomato ketchup
☆ 60 g (2 oz) tuna, flaked, 5 ml (1 tsp) lemon juice and a little tartare sauce
☆ 60 g (2 oz) Cheddar or your favourite cheese, finely grated

PEANUT BUTTER FILLINGS

Peanut butter is an easy-to-use, nutritious spread but it does need some help to remain a favourite, so vary the way you use it. Try different breads: fruit or nut breads, wholemeal, rye and even Italian olive oil breads go well with peanut butter. If you family likes peanut butter, they're sure to love some of these ideas:

☆ peanut butter and honey
☆ peanut butter, honey and sliced bananas on fruit or nut bread
☆ peanut butter and grated carrots with raisins or sultanas
☆ peanut butter and apple sauce or grated apple on fruit or nut bread
☆ peanut butter and honey with fried, crumbled bacon
☆ peanut butter and cream cheese – add some jam for a special treat
☆ peanut butter and dill pickle slices on rye bread
☆ peanut butter with chopped dried fruits such as apricots or dates
☆ peanut butter, honey and thin pawpaw slices sprinkled with lemon juice
☆ peanut butter, honey and thinly sliced tinned or fresh peaches

POULTRY FILLINGS

Leftover chicken or turkey can be turned into satisfying sandwiches. Here's a basic recipe and some interesting variations:

SLICED CHICKEN WITH RELISH ❄

1 bread roll or 2 slices bread
parsley butter (see Bread Spreads, page 21)
slices of cold cooked chicken
30 ml (2 tbsp) sweetcorn relish

Butter each half of the roll or each slice of bread evenly with parsley butter. Stack slices of chicken on the bottom half and top with relish and remaining bread. Wrap well and chill until ready to pack.
SERVES 1.

TURKEY AND CRANBERRY ROLLS ❄

1 bread roll
chive butter (see Bread spreads, page 21)
slices of cold cooked turkey
30 ml (2 tbsp) cranberry sauce

Butter each half of the roll evenly with chive butter. Place a few slices of turkey on the bottom half. Add cranberry sauce and a few more turkey slices, and top with the remaining half of the roll. Wrap well and chill until ready to pack.
SERVES 1.

CHICKEN-FILLED PITTAS

A hot 'sandwich', ideal for cold winter's days.

30 ml (2 tbsp) sultanas
boiling water
30 ml (2 tbsp) chopped onion
15 ml (1 tbsp) butter or margarine
250 g (9 oz) cooked chicken, diced
75 ml (5 tbsp) condensed cream of chicken soup
60 g (2 oz) cooked peas
60 ml (4 tbsp) soured cream
15 ml (1 tbsp) milk
2.5 ml (½ tsp) curry powder or to taste
1 large Pitta bread (page 18), cut in half

Cover sultanas with boiling water and allow to stand for 5 minutes. Drain and set aside. In a saucepan, cook onion in butter or margarine until tender but not brown. Remove from heat, add chicken, soup, peas, soured cream, milk, curry powder and sultanas. Heat through, then divide mixture between two insulated containers that have been rinsed with boiling water. With each container, pack half the pitta bread in a sandwich bag. At lunch time, spoon the warm chicken mixture into pitta. Add crisp celery and crunchy carrot sticks to much with the sandwich.
SERVES 2.

Top to bottom: Peanut butter filling, Ham salad spread, Basic egg salad, Tuna salad and meat and cheese filling

CHICKEN SALAD ❋

250 g (9 oz) cooked chicken, minced
1 small dill pickle or gherkin, finely
  chopped
1 stick celery, finely chopped
45–60 ml (3–4 tbsp) mayonnaise
15 ml (1 tbsp) finely chopped onion
salt and pepper to taste

Mix chicken with the remaining ingredients.
Keep refrigerated until needed.
MAKES ABOUT 375 G (13 OZ).

**Try adding one of the following to the
basic sandwich:**
☆ bean or other sprouts
☆ tomato slices and shredded lettuce,
packed separately
☆ chopped apple, sprinkled with a little
lemon juice, and flaked almonds
☆ chopped ham and sliced green olives
☆ grated apple, a few drops of lemon
juice, a few sultanas and a pinch of curry
powder
☆ grated cheese and lettuce

SPICY CHICKEN TACOS

4 Tacos (page 21)

SALSA
1 large ripe tomato, chopped
1 small green pepper, finely chopped
1 small onion, finely chopped
2.5 ml (½ tsp) chilli powder or to taste
dash Tabasco
salt to taste

FILLING
250 g (9 oz) cooked chicken, diced
45 ml (3 tbsp) chopped pitted ripe olives
1 ripe avocado, peeled and diced
10 ml (2 tsp) lemon juice
60 ml (4 tbsp) soured cream
60 g (2 oz) Cheddar cheese, grated

To make salsa, combine tomato, green pepper, onion, chilli powder, Tabasco and salt in a
small bowl. Mix well, then chill. For filling,
combine chicken, olives, avocado and lemon
juice and toss to mix. Mix in soured cream and
chill. To pack, divide chicken mixture between
two plastic containers. Top each with half the
salsa and half the grated cheese. Seal. Pack
2 tacos into each of two plastic bags. At lunch
time, spoon mixture into taco shells. Remember to pack a paper plate and plastic knife and
fork as this sandwich will be messy to eat with
your fingers.
SERVES 2.

FISH FILLINGS
*Fish, especially the canned variety, makes
convenient, tasty fillings. Keep a few cans in
store and try some of these new ideas:*

TUNA OR SALMON SALAD ❋

200 g (7 oz) canned tuna or salmon,
  drained
45–60 ml (3–4 tbsp) mayonnaise
10 ml (2 tsp) lemon juice
15 ml (1 tbsp) finely chopped onion
30 ml (2 tbsp) chopped gherkin
3 hard-boiled egg yolks, finely sieved

Flake tuna or salmon and mix with all other
ingredients.
MAKES ABOUT 225 G (8 OZ), OR ENOUGH FOR
3 SANDWICHES.

**Here's how to give your fish sandwich
that something extra. Add:**
☆ sliced cucumber, packed separately
☆ sliced tomatoes, packed separately
☆ 15 ml (1 tbsp) sunflower or 10 ml (2 tsp)
toasted sesame seeds
☆ a few bean sprouts
☆ sliced hard-boiled egg
☆ sliced avocado sprinkled with lemon
juice and freshly ground black pepper
☆ a little grated carrot
☆ a little finely chopped celery
☆ 15 ml (1 tbsp) chutney
☆ a thin slice of cheese or a little grated
cheese of your choice

OTHER FISHY IDEAS
**Combine mashed sardines or pilchards
with:**
☆ chopped celery, lemon juice and a little
mayonnaise
☆ prepared horseradish, a little vinegar,
chopped onion and a little mayonnaise
☆ a little tomato ketchup and chopped
gherkin

**Combine mashed anchovies or fish
paste with:**
☆ chopped or sieved hard-boiled egg yolk
and mayonnaise
☆ a little tartare sauce, lettuce and
tomato
☆ finely chopped celery, onion, dill pickle
and a little lemon juice

**Combine boned and flaked smoked
mackerel with:**
☆ soured cream and chopped chives or
spring onions
☆ finely chopped hard-boiled egg,
mayonnaise and soaked sultanas
☆ cress and mayonnaise

TUNA POOR BOYS

2 long individual bread rolls, wholemeal
  or plain
15 ml (1 tbsp) oil
2.5 ml (½ tsp) garlic powder

FILLING
1 tomato, thinly sliced
½ green pepper, cut in thin strips
½ onion, thinly sliced
100 g (3½ oz) canned tuna, drained and
  flaked
6 large ripe olives, pitted and halved
4 canned anchovy fillets, drained
30 ml (2 tbsp) wine vinegar
pepper to taste

Halve rolls and remove a little of the soft bread
from both halves of each roll. Brush cut sides
with oil and sprinkle with garlic powder. Layer
bottom half of each roll with tomato, green
pepper, onion, tuna, olives and 2 anchovies.
Sprinkle with vinegar and season with pepper. Cover each with the top of the roll and cut
in half for easy eating. Wrap each roll well,
then weight with a heavy object for about 30
minutes. Refrigerate until ready to pack.
SERVES 2.

SALMON AND EGG OPEN
SANDWICH

1 slice rye bread, buttered
1 hard-boiled egg, sliced
60 g (2 oz) canned salmon, drained and
  flaked
freshly ground black pepper
30 ml (2 tbsp) soured cream
2.5 ml (½ tsp) lemon juice
pinch dried dill

Place bread in plastic container. Top with
slices of egg, then with salmon and sprinkle
with pepper. Cover container and chill until
ready to pack. Mix soured cream, lemon juice
and dill and pack separately. At lunch time,
pour cream mixture over salmon and eat with
a knife and fork.
SERVES 1.

VEGETARIAN FILLINGS
Good ideas for those who don't eat meat!

**Cottage cheese and sliced pear on fruit
or nut bread**
**Baked beans and apple on wholemeal
bread** For each serving, drain 90 ml (6
tbsp) baked beans and mix with 15 ml (1
tbsp) mayonnaise. Spread on buttered

wholemeal bread. Top with several thin slices of apple, brushed with lemon juice. Top with buttered wholemeal bread.

Salad sandwich For each serving, shred ¼ courgette and 30 g (1 oz) Cheddar cheese. Toss with a few bean sprouts, 15 ml (1 tbsp) lemon juice and salt and pepper to taste. Mound on buttered wholemeal bread and top with another slice. Pack natural yoghurt or soured cream to add at lunch time.

Waldorf salad filling For each serving, mix together 1 grated apple, 30 ml (2 tbsp) chopped walnuts, 15 ml (1 tbsp) raisins, 30 ml (2 tbsp) chopped celery, 45 ml (3 tbsp) chopped pineapple, 45 ml (3 tbsp) mayonnaise. Pack into a plastic container and add shredded lettuce.
SERVES 4–5.

BEAN SPROUT AND AVOCADO SALAD IN PITTA POCKETS

2 Pitta breads (page 18)
60 ml (4 tbsp) curd cheese

FILLING
1 avocado, peeled
10 ml (2 tsp) lemon juice
60 g (2 oz) bean sprouts
60 g (2 oz) shredded lettuce
1 small tomato, diced
30 ml (2 tbsp) Green goddess dip
  (page 10)
30 ml (2 tbsp) soured cream

Halve pittas and spread each half with some of the curd cheese. Place two halves in each of two sandwich bags and seal. To make filling, dice avocado flesh and coat well with lemon juice. In a bowl, mix avocado, bean sprouts, lettuce and tomato. Mix Green goddess dip and soured cream and add to avocado mixture. Toss lightly to mix. Divide mixture between two plastic containers and seal. At lunch time, spoon some of the salad mixture into each pitta half.
SERVES 2.

GREEK PITTAS

2 Pitta breads (page 18)
125 g (4 oz) shredded lettuce

Spicy chicken tacos make unusual sandwiches

FILLING
300 g (11 oz) canned chick peas, drained
2 spring onions, thinly sliced, including
  some of the top
½ cucumber, coarsely chopped
1 small tomato, coarsely chopped
125 g (4 oz) feta cheese, cut into cubes

DRESSING
60 ml (4 tbsp) oil (part olive oil,
  if desired)
30 ml (2 tbsp) vinegar
good pinch freshly ground black pepper
good pinch salt
good pinch dried oregano

Mix chick peas, onions, cucumber, tomato and cheese in a large bowl. In a small bowl or covered jar, beat ingredients for the dressing until well blended. Pour over chick pea mixture and toss to mix. Pack into two containers and top with half the lettuce. Cut a little off the top of each pitta bread. Pack in plastic bags. At lunch time, mix lettuce into filling and spoon into pitta. Pack some ripe olives to eat with the pitta.
SERVES 2.

MEAT FILLINGS
Leftover cooked meats make marvellous sandwich fillings. Here are ideas for cold meats – and lots of new flavours for the old standby, a ham sandwich:

HAM SALAD SPREAD

400 g (14 oz) cooked ham
2 sticks celery, finely chopped
75 ml (5 tbsp) mayonnaise or
  salad cream
5 ml (1 tsp) prepared horseradish
  or mustard
30 ml (2 tbsp) chopped gherkin

Mince cooked ham and turn into a large bowl. Add celery, mayonnaise or salad cream, horseradish or mustard and gherkin. Mix well and refrigerate until needed.
MAKES ABOUT 500 ML (17 FL OZ) OR ENOUGH FOR ABOUT 6 SANDWICHES.

Now, enhance the flavour by adding any of the following:
☆ a slice of Gruyère cheese and a crisp lettuce leaf
☆ a little cottage cheese and a few plump raisins
☆ a little well-drained crushed pineapple and a few chopped pecan nuts
☆ a little crumbled blue cheese and some finely chopped onion
☆ sieved egg yolk, a few drops of vinegar and a pinch of dried mixed herbs

MORE IDEAS WITH HAM

Ham on rye with garlic butter
(see Bread spreads, page 21).
Ham and baked beans on pumpernickel
For each serving, drain and mash 60 ml (4 tbsp) baked beans, add 15 ml (1 tbsp) pickle and prepared mustard to taste. Butter 2 slices of pumpernickel bread with mustard butter (see Bread spreads, page 21), spread bean mixture over bottom slice, add sliced ham and top with bread. Pack lettuce separately to add before eating.
Ham and potato salad Butter a bread roll with cheese butter (see Bread spreads, page 21). Add 60 ml (4 tbsp) potato salad, ham and dill pickle slices.
Ham and marmalade Make ham sandwiches with buttered raisin bread spread with orange marmalade.

ROAST BEEF AND CHUTNEY ROLL ❄

1 bread roll
horseradish butter (see Bread Spreads, page 21)
15 ml (1 tbsp) soured cream
slices of cold roast beef
15 ml (1 tbsp) chutney

Butter each half of the roll with horseradish butter. Spread with soured cream. Pile roast beef slices on bottom of roll. Add chutney and top with remaining half of the roll. Wrap and freeze if desired.
SERVES 1.

MEAT TORTILLA ROLL

1 Mexican tortilla, about 15 cm (6 inches) in diameter (page 21)

FILLING
30 ml (2 tbsp) curd cheese
5 ml (1 tsp) chopped chives
2.5 ml (½ tsp) prepared horseradish or mustard
pinch pepper
3 slices cold, cooked meat, such as roast beef, corned beef or lamb
1 small tomato, thinly sliced
2–3 lettuce or spinach leaves

Very lightly brush both sides of tortilla with water and place on a board. Mix curd cheese with chives, horseradish or mustard and pepper. Spread over one side of tortilla. Layer meat, tomato, lettuce or spinach on top, then roll tortilla up. Wrap in clingfilm and chill until ready to pack.
SERVES 1.

MEAT SALAD PITTAS

2 Pitta breads (page 18)

FILLING
150 g (5 oz) corned beef or other cold cooked meat
15 ml (1 tbsp) chopped green pepper
15 ml (1 tbsp) chopped onion
2.5 ml (½ tsp) celery salt
pepper to taste
2 hard-boiled eggs, chopped
45 ml (3 tbsp) mayonnaise
5 ml (1 tsp) prepared mustard
shredded lettuce
2 slices tomato

Chop meat and add green pepper, onion, celery salt, pepper, eggs, mayonnaise and mustard. Mix well and pack into two plastic containers. Top each with shredded lettuce and a tomato slice. Cover and chill until ready to pack. Slice off the top of each pitta and pack into plastic bags. At lunch time, spoon shredded lettuce, the tomato slice and meat mixture into the pitta. The filling can be prepared the night before and refrigerated until ready to pack.
SERVES 2.

VARIATION
This filling is equally delicious in tortillas.

BUNNY CHOW

Bunny chow is a traditional Natal 'take-away' made up of a hollowed out half-loaf of bread filled with a curry mixture. The name is a corruption of the Hindu word bhannia *meaning 'shopkeeper caste' and the Chinese word* chow *meaning 'mixture of food'.*

1 medium onion, sliced
15 ml (1 tbsp) oil
2 cloves garlic, chopped
2 tomatoes, chopped
5 ml (1 tsp) curry powder
2.5 ml (½ tsp) turmeric
400 g (14 oz) minced beef
425 g (15 oz) baked beans, drained or 90 g (3 oz) frozen mixed vegetables

Fry onion in oil until golden. Add garlic, tomatoes, curry powder and turmeric and cook for a few minutes. Add the mince to the pan, stir to combine well, and simmer for 30 minutes. Add baked beans or frozen vegetables and cook for a further 10 minutes. Pack into hollowed out bread rolls or use to fill Rotis (page 20).
SERVES 6.

CORNED BEEF SANDWICHES

225 g (8 oz) corned beef, diced
2 hard-boiled eggs, diced
45 ml (3 tbsp) chopped celery
30 ml (2 tbsp) chopped dill pickle
30 ml (2 tbsp) crushed, drained pineapple
5 ml (1 tsp) chopped chives
French dressing to moisten
8 slices wholemeal bread
sliced tomato

Combine the corned beef, diced eggs, chopped celery, dill pickle, pineapple and chives and mix thoroughly. Moisten with French dressing and spread on 4 slices of buttered wholemeal bread. Top with remaining slices of bread and wrap well. Pack sliced tomato separately to add to the sandwiches at lunch time.
SERVES 4.

DON'T FORGET THESE GREAT MEAT IDEAS

Here are some tasty flavour combinations using canned and processed cooked meats:

Canned corned beef or liver-sausage spread with:
☆ grated onion and chopped gherkin
☆ a little chopped cooked chicken or ham, chopped pickle and a little mayonnaise or sandwich spread
☆ prepared mustard and sliced tomato on rye bread
☆ prepared horseradish, pickle relish and a little orange juice just to moisten

Sliced luncheon meats, sliced tongue, chopped liver or salami with:
☆ grated cheese of your choice and pickle or chutney
☆ sieved hard-boiled egg and minced onion mixed with a little chutney
☆ grated cheese of your choice, sliced tomato and lettuce
☆ lettuce and cucumber
☆ a little drained, crushed pineapple, mixed with a little sandwich spread

Yeast or beef extract with:
☆ crunchy peanut butter
☆ grated cheese of your choice, crispy bacon and a little chutney
☆ grated cheese of your choice and Basic egg salad (page 12)
☆ thinly sliced onion and a sprinkling of sugar (the anti-social lunch special)
☆ cottage cheese, cucumber slices and freshly ground black pepper
☆ banana slices and French mustard
☆ cream cheese and tomato slices

INCREDIBLE BREADS

It's easy to use the same standard loaf of white, brown or wholemeal bread to make sandwiches every morning, but it's just as easy for your family to become bored with eating the same bread every lunch time.

Consult the list below and you could serve a different kind of bread for lunch every day for at least a month.

Bagels Glossy and doughnut-shaped, these firm, chewy bread rolls make a good base for cheese, cream cheese and meat sandwiches.

Baguettes Crusty French bread to slice in thin diagonals for sandwiches, or send with cheese, pâté and spreads. Or pack a hunk to tear into bite-sized pieces and eat with soups, stews or salads.

Bread sticks You can't turn them into a sandwich, but they're good to tuck into the lunch box for snacks or eating with soup, casseroles and salads.

Crispbreads and savoury biscuits You can make a sandwich – but if they are filled too long in advance, you'll have a soggy lunch. Much better to pack these separately and then top with a dip, a pâté or other spread at lunch time. Don't forget to add crispbread or biscuits to eat with soups and salads.

Croissants Flaky crescent-shaped French rolls that make great companions to hot soups, salads or pâtés.

Mexican tortillas (page 21) Versatile unleavened rounds of bread to spread with your favourite filling and roll or fold.

Pitta bread (page 18) The pitta bread is a favourite in the Middle East where it is stuffed with a variety of fillings. Cut each puffy pitta in half to make two holders for sandwich filling.

Rotis (page 20) Indian flat breads cooked in a pan or on a griddle until speckled and golden. They are often served filled with curry and rolled up.

OTHER INCREDIBLE BREADS

Wholemeal bread (page 18), date bread, Wholemeal banana bread (this page), Nut bread (page 20), a variety of bread rolls, Batter oat bread (page 18), Quick raisin loaf (page 18), pumpernickel, rye bread, White milk bread (this page), herb breads, yoghurt bread, health biscuits, Wheatgerm muffins (page 21), scones, English muffins and buttermilk bread.

WHITE MILK BREAD ❄

This white bread is made with milk for added nutrients.

1 kg (2¼ lb) strong plain white flour
30 ml (2 tbsp) fast-action dried yeast
800 ml (27 fl oz) milk
45 ml (3 tbsp) caster sugar
20 ml (4 tsp) butter or margarine
15 ml (1 tbsp) salt

Combine 350 g (12 oz) of the flour and the yeast in a large mixing bowl. Heat milk with sugar, butter or margarine and salt until just warm, stirring to melt butter. Add milk to dry ingredients in bowl. Beat with an electric mixer at low speed for about 30 seconds. Scrape down sides of bowl, then beat at high speed for about 3 minutes. Stir in enough of the remaining flour to make a moderately stiff dough. Knead dough for about 4 minutes with an electric mixer, or for about 10 minutes by hand. The dough should be smooth and elastic. Place in a large greased bowl, turning to grease dough. Stand in a warm place, covered, until dough has doubled in bulk, about 1½ hours. Punch down dough, turn out on a lightly floured surface and divide into three portions. Shape each portion into a smooth ball, cover, and rest for 10 minutes. Shape into loaves and place in three greased 23 x 13 cm (9 x 5 inch) loaf tins. Cover and stand in a warm place until doubled in bulk, 45–60 minutes. Bake at 190 °C (375 °F, gas 5) for about 45 minutes, or until golden brown. The loaf should sound hollow when tapped.
MAKES 3 LOAVES.

VARIATIONS
Bread rolls After the first rising, punch down and divide into three portions. Divide each portion into eight and shape each into a smooth ball. Place about 5 cm (2 inches) apart on a greased baking sheet. Allow to rise until nearly doubled in bulk, about 30 minutes, then flatten slightly with your hand. Bake at 190 °C (375 °F, gas 5) for 15–20 minutes, or until golden brown.

Cheesy bread Add 90 g (3 oz) Gruyère or Cheddar cheese, finely grated, 60 g (2 oz) Parmesan cheese, grated, and 2.5 ml (½ tsp) freshly ground black pepper to the mixture when stirring in remaining flour. Proceed as for basic White milk bread.

Onion and herb bread Add 30 ml (2 tbsp) chopped fresh herbs, such as dill, chives, thyme and parsley, 2.5 ml (½ tsp) freshly ground black pepper and 60 ml (4 tbsp) lightly sautéed onions to the mixture when stirring in the remaining flour. Proceed as above.

WHOLEMEAL BANANA BREAD ❄

100 g (3½ oz) caster sugar
175 ml (6 fl oz) fromage frais
30 ml (2 tbsp) butter or margarine
225 g (8 oz) bananas, mashed and peeled
2 eggs, beaten
125 g (4 oz) plain flour
7.5 ml (1½ tsp) baking powder
2.5 ml (½ tsp) bicarbonate of soda
5 ml (1 tsp) salt
125 g (4 oz) wholemeal flour
a little milk

Beat sugar with fromage frais and butter or margarine until light and fluffy. Add bananas and eggs and mix well. Sift together plain flour, baking powder, bicarbonate of soda and salt and mix with wholemeal flour. Stir into banana mixture, adding a little milk to make batter of a dropping consistency. Spoon batter into a greased 23 x 13 cm (9 x 5 inch) loaf tin and bake at 180 °C (350 °F, gas 4) for about 1 hour, or until firm and well risen. Turn out on a wire rack to cool. When cool, store bread well wrapped, or freeze.
MAKES 1 LOAF THAT CUTS INTO ABOUT 12 SLICES.

WHOLEMEAL BREAD ❊

575 g (1¼ lb) plain flour
30 ml (2 tbsp) fast-action dried yeast
700 ml (24 fl oz) water
100 g (3½ oz) soft brown sugar
60 g (2 oz) butter or margarine
15 ml (1 tbsp) salt
400 g (14 oz) wholemeal flour

In a large mixing bowl, combine 350 g (12 oz) of the plain flour and the yeast. In a saucepan, heat water, brown sugar, butter or margarine and salt until just warm, stirring to melt butter. Add this warm liquid to dry ingredients in bowl and beat at medium speed with an electric mixer until mixture is moistened, about 30 seconds. Scrape sides of bowl and then beat at high speed for 3 minutes. Add wholemeal flour and enough of the remaining plain flour to make a fairly stiff dough. Knead until smooth and elastic, about 10 minutes by hand or 4 minutes with an electric mixer. Place dough in a greased bowl, turning to grease the top then cover and leave to stand in a warm place until dough has almost doubled in bulk, about 45 minutes. Punch down, turn out on a lightly floured surface and shape into one large or two smaller loaves. Place in greased loaf tins and allow to rise, covered, in a warm place until doubled in bulk, about 45 minutes. Bake at 190 °C (375 °F, gas 5) for 40–45 minutes, until golden brown. The loaf should sound hollow when tapped. Remove from tins and cool on wire rack. When cool, wrap well and freeze if desired.
MAKES 1 LARGE OR 2 SMALL LOAVES.

VARIATIONS
Cheesy herb bread Add 90 g (3 oz) cheese, grated, and 5 ml (1 tsp) dried mixed herbs to the dry ingredients.
Wholewheat raisin bread Knead 150 g (5 oz) raisins into dough after the first rising.
Seed loaf Add 60 g (2 oz) sunflower seeds, 30 ml (2 tbsp) sesame seeds and 30 ml (2 tbsp) poppy seeds to dry ingredients.

BATTER OAT BREAD ❊

350 g (12 oz) plain flour
90 g (3 oz) rolled oats
15 ml (1 tbsp) fast-action dried yeast
300 ml (½ pint) milk
60 g (2 oz) butter or margarine
60 ml (4 tbsp) clear honey
10 ml (2 tsp) salt
1 egg
1 extra egg yolk, white reserved
30 ml (2 tbsp) rolled oats

Mix 175 g (6 oz) of the flour, 90 g (3 oz) rolled oats and yeast in a large mixing bowl. Heat milk with butter or margarine, honey and salt until just warm, stirring to melt butter. Add milk mixture to dry ingredients with egg and extra egg yolk. Beat in electric mixer at low speed for 30 seconds. Scrape down sides of bowl, then beat at high speed for 3 minutes. Mix in enough of the remaining flour to make a soft dough. Beat until smooth, about 2 minutes. Cover bowl and allow to rise in a warm place until doubled in bulk, about 1½ hours. Stir dough down with a wooden spoon. Grease a 2 litre (3½ pint) ovenproof dish and sprinkle with 15 ml (1 tbsp) rolled oats. Turn dough into dish and allow to rise in a warm place for about 45 minutes, or until doubled in bulk. Brush top with beaten egg white and sprinkle with remaining rolled oats. Bake at 190 °C (375 °F, gas 5) for 40–45 minutes, or until loaf sounds hollow when tapped on base. Leave bread to stand for about 15 minutes, then remove to a wire rack to cool. When cool, wrap well and freeze if desired.
MAKES 1 LOAF.

QUICK WHOLEMEAL LOAF ❊

250 g (9 oz) wholemeal flour
7.5 ml (1½ tsp) bicarbonate of soda
5 ml (1 tsp) salt
20 ml (4 tsp) wheatgerm
1 egg
15 ml (1 tbsp) clear honey
30 ml (2 tbsp) oil
250 ml (8 fl oz) buttermilk
a few sunflower or sesame seeds
** (optional)**

Mix wholemeal flour, bicarbonate of soda, salt and wheatgerm in a mixing bowl. Combine egg, honey, oil and buttermilk and add to dry ingredients. Mix until ingredients are well moistened, then spoon into a greased 23 x 13 cm (9 x 5 inch) loaf tin and sprinkle with seeds, if desired. Bake at 190 °C (375 °F, gas 5) for 50–55 minutes, or until a skewer inserted in the centre comes out clean. Turn out on a wire rack and cool. When cool, wrap well and freeze if desired.
MAKES 1 LOAF THAT WILL CUT INTO 10–12 SLICES.

VARIATION
Quick herb and cheese loaf Add 5 ml (1 tsp) dried mixed herbs and 60 g (2 oz) cheese of your choice, grated, to the dry ingredients.

PITTA BREAD

Pitta bread is a large, flat round of bread that puffs up during baking to form a hollow shell. When cooled and split in half, each half forms a pocket, an edible holder for sandwich fillings. Select ideas for pitta fillings from the egg, cheese, meat, poultry or fish sections in 'The Great Sandwich' (pages 11–16).

175–250 ml (6–8 fl oz) warm water
15 ml (1 tbsp) fast-action dried yeast
15 ml (1 tbsp) caster sugar
325 g (11½ oz) plain flour
5 ml (1 tsp) salt
5 ml (1 tsp) oil

Combine 60 ml (4 tbsp) of the warm water with yeast and sugar. Stir to dissolve yeast, then leave to stand in a warm place until bubbly, about 5 minutes. Sift flour with salt and place in a mixing bowl. Add oil, then yeast mixture to dry ingredients and beat at medium speed with an electric mixer until well combined, about 1 minute. With mixer running, add enough of the remaining warm water to make the dough form a ball. Turn out on a lightly floured surface and knead until smooth and elastic, 5–8 minutes. Allow dough to rise, covered, in a warm place for 45–60 minutes, or until doubled in bulk. Punch dough down. Divide into 10 parts and roll each into a ball. Roll each ball out very thinly on a lightly floured surface to form a 15 cm (6 inch) circle. Place dough circles on lightly greased baking sheets and cover loosely. Leave to stand in a warm place for 25 minutes. Heat oven to 200 °C (400 °F, gas 6) and bake pittas about 7 minutes, or until puffed and golden brown. Remove to wire rack and allow to cool. Carefully cut pockets in half and fill as desired. Pittas can be stored in a container with a tightly fitting lid for several days.
MAKES 10–12 PITTAS.

> *NOTE: Remember to pack the empty pitta separately from the filling in your lunch box. Place pitta bread in a plastic sandwich bag and filling in a plastic container. Pack shredded lettuce on top of filling in the plastic container; it will add crispness to the finished sandwich. At lunch time, spoon the filling and lettuce into the pitta.*

Clockwise from left: Wheatgerm muffins, Wholemeal banana bread and freshly baked Nut bread

NUT BREAD ❄

Use the bread for chicken or ham sandwiches.

350 g (12 oz) plain flour
200 g (7 oz) granulated sugar
20 ml (4 tsp) baking powder
5 ml (1 tsp) salt
1 egg, beaten
375 ml (13 fl oz) milk
60 ml (4 tbsp) oil
125 g (4 oz) nuts (walnuts, pecans or
   hazel nuts), chopped

Sift the dry ingredients into a mixing bowl. Combine egg, milk and oil and add to dry ingredients. Mix well, then stir in nuts. Spoon the mixture into a well-greased 23 x 13 cm (9 x 5 inch) loaf tin and bake at 190 °C (375 °F, gas 5) for about 60 minutes, or until a skewer inserted in the centre comes out clean. Remove bread from tin and cool on a wire rack. When cool, wrap well and freeze if desired.
MAKES 1 LOAF THAT CUTS INTO 10–12 SLICES.

VARIATION
Add about 90 g (3 oz) Cheddar cheese, grated, to the batter with the nuts.

ROTIS

Rotis are rounds of unleavened bread, similar to Mexican tortillas, that are delicious with meat or vegetable fillings. Although Hindu in origin, they are popular in Britain too.

250 g (9 oz) plain flour
5 ml (1 tsp) salt
15 ml (1 tbsp) oil
125 ml (4 fl oz) water
60 ml (4 tbsp) softened margarine
60 ml (4 tbsp) plain flour
oil for frying

Sift the flour and salt into a mixing bowl and add oil and enough water to make a soft dough. Knead lightly, then cut into six pieces. Roll out each piece into a 23 cm (9 inch) circle, spread with a little soft margarine and sprinkle with flour. Roll up and twist into a ball, then rest for 30 minutes or freeze for later use. Roll out the balls of dough to 18 cm (7 inch) circles and gently fry in a little oil until freckled golden on both sides. Cover generously with filling – try Bunny chow (page 16) – and fold or roll up for easy eating.
MAKES 6 ROTIS.

APRICOT BRAN BREAD ❄

100 g (3½ oz) dried apricots, finely
   chopped
boiling water
45 ml (3 tbsp) soft brown sugar
175 g (6 oz) plain flour
100 g (3½ oz) caster sugar
15 ml (1 tbsp) baking powder
5 ml (1 tsp) salt
pinch ground allspice
90 g (3 oz) bran flakes
250 ml (8 fl oz) milk
2 eggs, beaten
75 ml (5 tbsp) oil

Place apricots in a small bowl and add boiling water to just cover. Stand for 10 minutes, then drain well and add brown sugar. Sift flour with white sugar, baking powder, salt and allspice. Mix cereal with milk, eggs and oil. Add cereal mixture to dry ingredients, mixing to just moisten. Carefully stir in apricot mixture. Spoon into a greased loaf tin and sprinkle top with a little additional brown sugar, if desired. Bake at 190 °C (375 °F, gas 5) for 50–55 minutes. turn out on a wire rack to cool. When cool, wrap well and freeze if desired.
MAKES 1 LOAF THAT CUTS INTO 10–12 SLICES.

Rotis filled with Bunny chow make a satisfying winter meal

Make up savoury butters with orange or mint, chives or dill or even garlic

MEXICAN TORTILLAS ❊

Tortillas are flat, unleavened rounds of bread. They make good holders for a wide variety of fillings, and are just folded over or rolled up with the filling. A taco is a tortilla that has been fried in oil and folded into a U-shape while still warm. It is crisp and can hold a lot of flavourful filling.

150 g (5 oz) plain flour
15 g (½ oz) cornmeal
60 g (2 oz) cornflour
2.5 ml (½ tsp) salt
5 ml (1 tsp) baking powder
45 ml (3 tbsp) margarine
125 ml (4 fl oz) water

Sift dry ingredients into a mixing bowl. Cut margarine in pieces and rub into flour mixture. Add enough water to make a soft but not sticky dough. Turn out on a lightly floured surface and knead until smooth and elastic, about 5 minutes. Shape enough dough into six balls and leave to stand, covered, for about 20 minutes. Roll each ball out on a lightly floured surface to an 18 cm (7 inch) circle. Cook tortillas in a hot, ungreased, heavy frying pan or griddle. Cook until lightly flecked with brown on one side, about 60 seconds, then turn and cook on other side. When all the tortillas have been cooked and cooled, stack them with double layers of waxed paper in between and place in a plastic bag. Seal well and freeze. To use, remove as many tortillas as needed and thaw for a few minutes, then cover with filling and fold over or roll up.

Tacos Fry cooked tortilla in a little hot oil, then fold into a U-shape, drain and allow to dry. Pack the sandwich filling into this crispy holder.
MAKES 6 TORTILLAS OR TACOS.

NOTE: For easy rolling of tortilla with filling, dampen both sides of tortilla slightly and allow to stand a few minutes before rolling.

WHEATGERM MUFFINS ❊

Delicious with a cream cheese or fruit filling and a salad.

175 g (6 oz) plain flour
60 ml (4 tbsp) caster sugar
10 ml (2 tsp) baking powder
5 ml (1 tsp) salt
125 g (4 oz) wheatgerm
2.5 ml (½ tsp) ground cinnamon
1 egg, well beaten
200 ml (7 fl oz) milk
60 g (2 oz) butter or margarine, melted
60 ml (4 tbsp) molasses

Sift flour, sugar, baking powder and salt into a mixing bowl. Stir in wheatgerm and cinnamon. Combine egg, milk, melted butter or margarine and molasses and add to dry ingredients. Stir until mixture is just moistened. Do not overmix, as the batter should still be lumpy. Spoon batter into 12 greased muffin tins, filling each tin about three-quarters full. Bake at 200 °C (400 °F, gas 6) for 20 minutes. Remove muffins from tins and cool on a wire rack. When cool, wrap well and freeze if desired.
MAKES 12 MUFFINS.

VARIATIONS
Cheesy muffins For a savoury treat, omit the cinnamon and stir 60 g (2 oz) grated Cheddar cheese into dry ingredients. Proceed as described above.
Nutty muffins Add 60 g (2 oz) chopped pecan nuts or walnuts to dry ingredients. Proceed as described above.

BREAD SPREADS

You can change a very ordinary sandwich into an exceptional eating experience by spreading the bread with butter or margarine that is just that little bit different. These spreads don't take long to make, but they do make a great flavour difference. Mix any of the following into 125 g (4 oz) butter:

☆ 30 ml (2 tbsp) chopped fresh parsley. Use on savoury sandwiches.
☆ 20 ml (4 tsp) chopped chives. Adds flavour to chicken, cheese, cottage cheese and meat sandwiches.
☆ 10 ml (2 tsp) dried dill. Good with cream cheese, cottage cheese, curd cheese and fish sandwiches.
☆ 5 ml (1 tsp) dried tarragon. Spread on bread for chicken or fish fillings.
☆ 5–7.5 ml (1–1½ tsp) curry powder. Goes well with chicken or meat fillings.
☆ 5 ml (1 tsp) dry mustard. Use with ham or other meat fillings.
☆ 45 ml (3 tbsp) grated cheese of your choice. This will be a delicious accompaniment to cream cheese, meat, and even to peanut butter.
☆ 15 ml (1 tbsp) grated orange or lemon rind. Adds an unusual flavour to sandwiches containing raisins, apples or peanut butter.
☆ 30 ml (2 tbsp) tomato ketchup or chilli sauce. A tangy touch for chicken or meat sandwiches.
☆ 7.5–10 ml (1½–2 tsp) prepared horseradish. Great with roast meat sandwiches.
☆ 10 ml (2 tsp) chopped fresh mint. Use for cold roast lamb sandwiches.
☆ 1–2 cloves garlic, crushed.

THE MAIN COURSE

What is a bolognese doing in a lunch box? Proving a nutritious hot lunch! Yes, you can pack soups, stews, casseroles, quiches and pizzas to take to work or school. Thermos containers, which keep foods hot or cold, come in various shapes and sizes and don't have to be expensive. The wide-mouthed, insulated containers are particularly useful – they're easy to pack and the contents can be transferred to a plate, mug or bowl at lunch time and be eaten with a spoon or fork.

Many of the recipes given in this chapter can be frozen, so prepare several dishes and solve the main-course problem for weeks to come. Divide into individual portions, spoon into foil or plastic freezer containers, (see 'Fill the Freezer', pages 54–59 for guide-lines on freezing), then reheat in time to pack. There are also suggestions for what to serve with each dish.

CHILLI CON CARNE ❅

Serve this spicy, thick 'soup' with dill pickles and vegetable sticks and add Orange and banana fruit salad (page 42) for dessert.

15 ml (1 tbsp) oil
450 g (1 lb) minced beef
½ small onion, chopped
30 ml (2 tbsp) cornmeal
45 ml (3 tbsp) chopped green pepper
425 g (15 oz) canned red kidney beans
400 g (14 oz) canned whole tomatoes
30 ml (2 tbsp) chilli powder
5 ml (1 tsp) salt
2.5 ml (½ tsp) ground cumin
2.5 ml (½ tsp) dried oregano
good pinch garlic powder

Heat oil in a large frying pan and add minced beef and onion. Cook, stirring occasionally, until meat loses its red colour. Stir in cornmeal, then remaining ingredients, including the liquid from canned kidney beans and tomatoes, and bring to the boil. Reduce heat and simmer, covered, for 30 minutes, stirring occasionally. Cool, then refrigerate for up to 3 days. To freeze, spoon chilled mixture into individual containers and place in freezer. Thaw overnight in the refrigerator, then reheat desired amount, check flavouring, and spoon into a wide-mouthed thermos and seal.
SERVES 4.

Versatile pizzas make tasty lunch-time treats

PIZZA ❅

These individual pizzas make a filling lunch when packed with salad.

SCONE PIZZA DOUGH
60 g (2 oz) butter
250 g (9 oz) self-raising flour
5 ml (1 tsp) salt
60 ml (4 tbsp) milk
1 egg

TOMATO SAUCE
1 large onion, finely chopped
1 clove garlic, finely chopped
15 ml (1 tbsp) oil
1 kg (2¼ lb) tomatoes, peeled and chopped
30 ml (2 tbsp) tomato paste
salt and pepper to taste
2.5 ml (½ tsp) dried oregano

TOPPING
175 g (6 oz) mozzarella, Gruyère or Cheddar cheese, grated

To make dough, rub butter into flour and salt until mixture resembles breadcrumbs. Combine milk and egg and stir into dry ingredients to form a soft dough. Turn out onto a lightly floured surface and knead gently two or three times. Quarter the dough and roll out each into a circle about 18 cm (7 inches) in diameter. Place the dough circles on a lightly greased baking sheet. To make tomato sauce, sauté onion and garlic in hot oil for a few minutes until onion is tender. Add tomatoes, tomato paste, seasoning and herbs and simmer, uncovered, until mixture is thick, 15–20 minutes. Spread tomato mixture over pizza bases and top with grated cheese. Bake at 200 °C (400 °F, gas 6) for 15–20 minutes, or until cooked. To freeze, cool, then wrap each individual pizza well, seal, label and place in the freezer. Thaw overnight in the refrigerator before packing for lunch.
MAKES 4 INDIVIDUAL PIZZAS.

PIZZA ADDITIONS
Add one of the following ingredients to the pizza before topping with the grated cheese – or use several to make an interesting combination.

Anchovy fillets
Pitted black olives
Chopped cooked bacon
Chopped cooked ham
Chopped green pepper
Sautéed, sliced mushrooms
Well-drained, flaked tuna
Cooked shrimps or prawns
Cooked, well-seasoned minced beef
Thin slices or strips of salami
Sliced cooked sausages
Drained pineapple chunks
Diced cooked chicken
Drained asparagus spears
Sliced gherkins
Feta cheese
Sliced tomatoes
Chopped celery
Onion rings
Garlic
Chilli
Sliced artichoke hearts
Capers

Meat loaf served with Horseradish sauce and Waldorf salad

LEMONY SALMON AND RICE CASSEROLE

Pack with a salad and fresh fruit.

225 g (8 oz) canned salmon
400 g (14 oz) canned cream of celery
  soup
125 ml (4 fl oz) water
150 g (5 oz) long-grain rice
60 ml (4 tbsp) dry sherry
½ small onion, chopped
2.5 ml (½ tsp) dried dill
salt and lemon pepper to taste
juice of ½ large lemon

Place salmon and juices in an ovenproof dish and flake coarsely with a fork. Add undiluted soup, water, rice, sherry and onion, and season with dill, salt and pepper. Stir in lemon juice and bake, covered, at 190 °C (375 °F, gas 5) for 25 minutes. Uncover and bake 8–10 minutes more. Chill and refrigerate for up to 3 days. To pack, reheat the desired amount, spoon into wide-mouthed thermos and seal.
SERVES 3–4.

MEAT LOAF ❄

Cut thick slices of meat loaf for a main course, or thin ones to make sandwich fillings. Serve with a tangy sauce (see Cold roast beef, pages 47–48) and a salad.

2 eggs
125 ml (4 fl oz) tomato juice
500 g (18 oz) minced beef
75 g (2½ oz) fresh breadcrumbs
45 ml (3 tbsp) finely chopped onion
15 ml (1 tbsp) chopped fresh parsley
salt and pepper to taste
5 ml (1 tsp) dried mixed herbs
2.5 ml (½ tsp) dry mustard
pinch garlic powder or garlic salt
60 g (2 oz) Cheddar cheese, grated

Break eggs into a large mixing bowl and add tomato juice. Mix well. Add beef and all the remaining ingredients. Mix lightly but thoroughly and press gently into a small, greased loaf tin. Bake, uncovered, at 190 °C (375 °F, gas 5) for 45 minutes. Allow to stand a few minutes. Slice, wrap and refrigerate for up to 4 days. To freeze, slice, chill and wrap individual slices, seal and label. Thaw overnight in the refrigerator before packing.
SERVES 4–6.

BARBECUED PORK SANDWICHES ❄

Here's a good way to use up leftover roast pork. Pack a fresh roll, a paper plate and don't forget the knife and fork. Crisp apple wedges, lightly sprinkled with lemon juice, complete the meal.

30 ml (2 tbsp) oil
½ small green pepper, seeded and
  chopped
30 ml (2 tbsp) chopped onion
250 g (9 oz) cooked pork, diced
175 ml (6 fl oz) tomato sauce
10 ml (2 tsp) prepared mustard
30 ml (2 tbsp) soft brown sugar
15 ml (1 tbsp) Worcestershire sauce
salt and pepper to taste

Heat oil in a large pan and sauté green pepper and onion until tender. Add pork, tomato sauce, mustard, brown sugar and Worcestershire sauce. Season with salt and pepper. Cook over low heat, stirring frequently, for about 15 minutes, or until thick. This mixture can be refrigerated for up to 4 days, or frozen in individual portions for up to 2 weeks. To pack, reheat desired amount and spoon into a wide-mouthed thermos. At lunch time, spoon over a buttered roll.

SERVES 6.

LEEK AND BACON QUICHE ✳

Serve this delicious quiche with a mixed salad and, for dessert, add fresh fruit of the season to make a balanced and satisfying meal.

PASTRY
300 g (11 oz) plain flour
5 ml (1 tsp) salt
2.5 ml (½ tsp) dried mixed herbs
175 g (6 oz) margarine
a little water

FILLING
175 g (6 oz) streaky bacon, rinds removed
2 leeks, thinly sliced
125 g (4 oz) Cheddar or Gruyère cheese, grated
3 eggs
250 ml (8 fl oz) milk
salt and pepper to taste
2.5 ml (½ tsp) dried mixed herbs

To make the pastry, mix flour, salt and herbs. Rub in margarine until mixture resembles fine breadcrumbs. Add enough water to form a soft dough. Roll out on a lightly floured surface and use to line four individual foil quiche dishes. To make the filling, chop bacon and cook in a heavy-based frying pan until lightly browned. Add leeks and cook until tender. Remove bacon and leeks from pan with a slotted spoon, draining well. Divide mixture between pastry shells. Reserve a quarter of the grated cheese, sprinkle remainder over leek and bacon mixture. Mix eggs, milk, salt, pepper and herbs. Carefully spoon egg mixture into pie shells. Sprinkle with reserved cheese. Bake at 190 °C (375 °F, gas 5) for about 30 minutes, or until filling has set. Cool on a wire rack. To freeze, wrap each pie individually, seal well and label. Freeze. Thaw overnight in the refrigerator before packing in the lunch box.

SERVES 4 AS A MAIN COURSE, OR 8 AS A SNACK.

CLASSIC CARBONNADE ✳

Serve this beef stew with crisp vegetable pieces and Yoghurt dill dip (page 10).

2 rashers bacon, rinds removed
1 large onion, sliced
750 g (1¾ lb) stewing beef, cut into 5 cm (2 inch) pieces
oil
15 ml (1 tbsp) plain flour
200 ml (7 fl oz) beer
125 ml (4 fl oz) water
1 beef stock cube
1 small bay leaf
5 ml (1 tsp) caster sugar
2.5 ml (½ tsp) dried thyme
salt and pepper to taste
15 ml (1 tbsp) red wine vinegar

Dice bacon, then cook in a large frying pan until well browned. Removed with a slotted spoon and reserve. Sauté onion in bacon fat until tender and lightly browned. Remove and reserve onion. Cook beef in remaining fat, a few pieces at a time, until well browned on all sides, stirring occasionally and adding a little oil if necessary. Remove meat pieces as they brown. Add 15 ml (1 tbsp) oil to pan, stir in flour and cook, stirring, until flour has browned. Gradually stir in beer and remaining ingredients, except vinegar, and cook, stirring, until slightly thickened. Place bacon, onion, beef and sauce in an ovenproof dish, stirring to mix. Bake in the oven at 180 °C (350 °F, gas 4) for about 1¾ hours, or until meat is tender. To serve at once, stir in wine vinegar. To freeze, omit vinegar, pack into individual freezer containers, seal and label. To serve, thaw and reheat, and add a little vinegar to each portion. Pack into wide-mouthed thermos for a hot lunch.

SERVES 4.

BEEFBURGER PASTIES ✳

Add vegetable sticks or Stuffed celery sticks (page 8), fruit and a Marshmallow cup-cake (page 50) for a hearty school lunch.

400 g (14 oz) frozen puff pastry, thawed
175 g (6 oz) minced beef
10 ml (2 tsp) prepared mustard
15 ml (1 tbsp) tomato ketchup
15 ml (1 tbsp) chopped pickled gherkin
60 g (2 oz) cheese of your choice, grated
salt and pepper to taste
few drops Worcester sauce
4 tomato slices
1 egg, beaten

Roll the pastry out to a square 5 mm (¼ inch) thick and cut into four squares. Mix beef with mustard, tomato ketchup, chopped gherkin, grated cheese, salt, pepper and Worcestershire sauce. Shape into four patties. Place a patty in the centre of each pastry square. Place a slice of tomato on top of each patty. Moisten edges of pastry and bring together to form a bundle. Seal edges well. Place on a baking sheet. Brush with beaten egg and bake at 200 °C (400 °F, gas 6) for about 25 minutes, or until golden brown. Allow to cool, then chill before packing. To freeze, open-freeze bundles before cooking, then wrap well, seal and label. Thaw overnight in refrigerator, then bake and pack as described above.

SERVES 4.

CHICKEN IN TOMATO PEPPER SAUCE ✳

Wholemeal bread and fresh fruit complete this meal.

2 whole chicken breasts, skinned and boned
30 ml (2 tbsp) oil
2 green peppers, seeded and cut into bite-sized pieces
1 onion, chopped
125 g (4 oz) mushrooms, sliced
225 g (8 oz) canned whole tomatoes, chopped, and juice
60 ml (4 tbsp) dry red wine
5 ml (1 tsp) caster sugar
2.5 ml (½ tsp) dried tarragon
5 ml (1 tsp) lemon juice
salt and pepper to taste

Cut chicken into bite-sized pieces and sauté in hot oil until lightly browned. Remove chicken to an ovenproof dish. Cook pepper, onion and mushrooms in remaining oil until peppers and onions are tender. Add tomatoes and remaining ingredients and heat through. Add to chicken and bake, uncovered, at 180 °C (350 °F, gas 4) for 20–30 minutes, or until chicken is tender. The chicken mixture can be refrigerated for up to 3 days, or frozen for up to 2 weeks. To pack, reheat desired amount, spoon into wide-mouthed thermos and seal.

SERVES 4.

> NOTE: This dish can be made with diced leftover cooked chicken. Make up vegetable mixture, add chicken and heat through.

MACARONI BOLOGNESE

Pack green salad and crispy breadsticks with this casserole.

125 g (4 oz) macaroni
30 ml (2 tbsp) oil
½ small onion, finely chopped
½ small carrot, finely chopped
1 small stick celery, thinly sliced
1 small clove garlic, finely chopped
250 g (9 oz) minced beef
125 g (4 oz) chicken livers, coarsely chopped
400 g (14 oz) canned whole tomatoes
90 ml (6 tbsp) tomato paste
60 ml (4 tbsp) water
30 ml (2 tbsp) dry red wine
salt and pepper to taste
2.5 ml (½ tsp) dried basil
2.5 (½ tsp) dried oregano

Prepare macaroni according to package directions. Drain, rinse and keep warm. Meanwhile, heat oil in a large saucepan and sauté onion, carrot, celery and garlic until tender, stirring frequently. Remove vegetables with a slotted spoon and reserve. Add beef to pan and cook, stirring, until meat just loses its pinkness. Add chicken livers and cook until just done. Add macaroni, cooked vegetables and remaining ingredients and heat until bubbling. Pack into wide-mouthed thermos flasks.
SERVES 2–3.

NOTE: This casserole can be made in advance and reheated. Cook the macaroni, vegetables and meat mixture. Combine and add remaining ingredients, then refrigerate. To use, heat the desired amount and pack for lunch.

SALMON LOAF ❋

Pack a generous slice with a small container of tomato sauce, a wedge of lemon and tomato wedges.

2 eggs
150 ml (¼ pint) milk
15 ml (1 tbsp) lemon juice
45 g (1½ oz) fresh breadcrumbs
45 ml (3 tbsp) finely chopped onion
15 ml (1 tbsp) finely chopped fresh parsley
salt and pepper to taste
10 ml (2 tsp) chopped chives
15 ml (1 tbsp) butter, melted
450 g (1 lb) canned salmon
paprika

Beat eggs and milk in a large bowl until well blended. Add lemon juice, breadcrumbs, onion, parsley, salt and pepper, chopped chives and butter. Flake salmon and add to mixture with liquid. Mix well and spread in a greased 23 cm (9 inch) pie dish. Sprinkle with paprika. Bake at 180 °C (350 °F, gas 4) for about 40 minutes, or until mixture is firm. Cool, then cut into wedges. Wrap and refrigerate for up to 3 days. To freeze, cool, then wrap individual slices, seal and label. Thaw overnight in the refrigerator before packing.
SERVES 6–8.

CHEESY VEGETABLE QUICHE ❋

Serve this quiche with a fruit drink and Orange coconut fingers (page 62).

CHEESE PASTRY
60 g (2 oz) butter
125 g (4 oz) plain flour
60 g (2 oz) Cheddar cheese, finely grated
2.5 ml (½ tsp) salt
1 egg yolk
a little water

FILLING
1 small onion, finely chopped
15 ml (1 tbsp) butter
2 tomatoes, peeled and sliced
5–6 mushrooms, sliced
3 eggs
90 g (3 oz) Cheddar cheese, grated
125 ml (4 fl oz) milk
100 ml (7 tbsp) single cream
1 carrot, grated
2.5 ml (½ tsp) dried mixed herbs
salt and pepper to taste

To make pastry, rub butter into flour and add cheese and salt. Mix egg yolk with about 30 ml (2 tbsp) water. Add enough egg mixture to dry ingredients to make a soft dough. Roll out and line a 23 cm (9 inch) pie or quiche dish. To make filling, sauté onion in butter until tender. Remove onion from pan with a slotted spoon, and spread over prepared pastry. Top with tomato slices, then mushroom slices. Mix eggs, grated cheese, milk, cream, carrot and herbs. Season with salt and pepper. Spoon over vegetables in pastry case and bake at 190 °C (375 °F, gas 5) for 30–35 minutes, or until filling has set. Cool on a wire rack, then cut into wedges and chill or freeze. To freeze, wrap individual slices and seal well. Label and freeze. Thaw overnight in the refrigerator before packing.
SERVES 6–8.

PILCHARD PIE ❋

Serve this savoury pie with Orange and carrot salad (page 39).

WHOLEMEAL PASTRY
150 g (5 oz) wholemeal flour
60 ml (4 tbsp) wheatgerm
2.5 ml (½ tsp) salt
90 g (3 oz) margarine
45 ml (3 tbsp) water

FILLING
200 g (7 oz) canned pilchards in tomato sauce
3 eggs
375 ml (13 fl oz) evaporated milk
1 small onion, finely chopped
125 g (4 oz) Gruyère cheese, grated
pinch cayenne pepper
good pinch dried marjoram
15 ml (1 tbsp) lemon juice

To make pastry, combine flour, wheatgerm and salt. Cut margarine into pieces and rub into dry ingredients. Add just enough water to form a stiff dough. Roll out and use to line six individual pie tins. To make filling, mash pilchards, then combine with all other ingredients. Spoon mixture into prepared pastry shells and bake at 180 °C (350 °F, gas 4) for about 30 minutes, or until filling has set. Cool on wire racks. Wrap well, seal, label and freeze. Thaw overnight in the refrigerator, then pack.
SERVES 6.

TOMATO BUTTERMILK BISQUE

This soup can be served hot or cold. To complete the lunch, add a Tuna salad sandwich (page 14) or cream cheese and walnuts on fruit bread, and round off with Raisin drop cookies (page 62).

400 g (14 oz) canned condensed tomato soup
500 ml (17 fl oz) buttermilk
150 ml (¼ pint) water
good pinch dried marjoram
15 ml (1 tbsp) chopped chives

Turn soup into a saucepan, stir in buttermilk, water and marjoram. Heat just to boiling, then immediately reduce heat and simmer, stirring occasionally, for 5 minutes. If serving hot, pour into wide-mouthed thermos flasks and seal. To serve cold, chill, then pour into thermos and seal. Add chives just before closing thermos flask.
SERVES 4.

THE EXECUTIVE LUNCH

Picture the busy executive at lunch time – a sandwich in one hand, financial report in the other. He, or she, may be deskbound with no time to go out in search of something for lunch, but will still need a well-balanced meal to provide energy for the afternoon's work. The executive lunch should be light but filling, high in energy and low in carbohydrates and fats. Organise the packed lunch to fit in a briefcase and keep a thermos handy for foods that must be kept hot or cold. Menu suggestions for well-balanced packed lunches for executives are provided in the box below.

EXECUTIVE LUNCH MENUS

*Chicken vegetable salad
    (this page)*
Wheatgerm muffin (page 21)
Fresh fruit

Apple and tuna salad (this page)
Pitta bread (page 18)
Pickles and olives

Salmon wine spread (page 28)
Pumpernickel or rye bread
Green salad
Fresh strawberries

Stuffed tomatoes (page 28)
Celery and carrot sticks
Crispbread
2 Coconut meringues (page 42)

Aubergine pâté (page 28)
Quick wholemeal loaf (page 18)
Five fruits salad (page 28)

Executive kebab (page 28)
Italian pasta salad (page 45)
Fresh fruit

---

*Salmon and egg open sandwich
    (page 14)*
Courgette salad (this page)
Fruit trifle (page 28)

Cold chicken
Bean salad (page 40)
*Fresh fruit salad (page 32) with
    Almond orange poundcake
    (page 50)*

---

*Chilled potato and leek soup
    (page 28)*
Cheese and bean sprout roll
Fresh fruit

CHICKEN VEGETABLE SALAD

125 g (4 oz) cooked chicken, diced
60 g (2 oz) frozen peas
60 g (2 oz) frozen green beans
30 ml (2 tbsp) chopped spring onion
15 ml (1 tbsp) wine vinegar
2.5 ml (½ tsp) dried tarragon
2.5 ml (½ tsp) caster sugar
pinch salt and pepper
good pinch prepared mustard
good pinch prepared horseradish
15 ml (1 tbsp) oil
few flaked almonds
lettuce leaves

Place chicken in a mixing bowl. Cook peas and beans in boiling water for 5 minutes, then drain and rinse in cold water. Drain again and add to chicken. Combine onion, vinegar, tarragon, sugar, salt and pepper, mustard, horseradish and oil in a small saucepan and bring to the boil. Reduce heat and simmer until onion is tender. Allow mixture to cool, then add to chicken. Add flaked almonds and toss lightly to mix. Turn the mixture into two containers with tightly fitting lids and chill. Pack into lunch box. Pack lettuce leaves separately. Provide a small plate or bowl and a knife and fork. At lunch time, place lettuce leaves on plate and top with chicken salad.
SERVES 2.

COURGETTE SALAD

2 medium courgettes, thinly sliced
30 ml (2 tbsp) chopped onion
a little chopped fresh dill
3 large white mushrooms, sliced
60 g (2 oz) blue cheese, crumbled
**60 ml (4 tbsp) Italian salad dressing (see
    Italian pasta salad, page 45)**
lettuce leaves

Combine courgettes, onion, dill, mushrooms and cheese and pour salad dressing over. Divide between two containers, seal well and chill. Pack the torn lettuce leaves separately and at lunch time, stir them into the salad.
SERVES 2.

APPLE AND TUNA SALAD

225 g (8 oz) carrots, finely grated
**1 small apple, peeled, cored and thinly
    sliced**
juice of 1 lemon
30 ml (2 tbsp) sultanas
2 oranges
2 sticks celery
200 g (7 oz) canned tuna, drained
10 ml (2 tsp) caster sugar
30 ml (2 tbsp) mayonnaise
45 ml (3 tbsp) chopped pecan nuts

Combine carrots and apple in a bowl and sprinkle with half the lemon juice. Cover sultanas with boiling water, allow to stand 1 minute, drain and add to carrot mixture. Peel oranges and divide into segments. Cut segments into bite-sized pieces and add to carrots. Finely chop celery and add to other ingredients in bowl. Flake the tuna and add to bowl. Combine sugar, mayonnaise and remaining lemon juice, mixing well. Add to the salad and toss lightly to mix. Divide the salad into two portions and place in plastic containers with tightly fitting lids. Chill until ready to pack. Just before packing, sprinkle each portion with chopped pecan nuts.
SERVES 2.

> *NOTE: This salad makes a super filling for a pitta. Pack separately, then spoon salad into pitta at lunch time.*

STUFFED TOMATOES

1 medium tomato
salt
90 ml (6 tbsp) Basic egg salad (page 12),
    Tuna salad (page 14), Ham salad
    spread (page 15) or Cheese filling
    (page 12)

Cut top from tomato and carefully scoop out
pulp. Save pulp for another purpose. Sprinkle
inside of tomato with salt and turn upside
down to drain for 15–20 minutes. Fill tomato
shell with selected filling and replace top.
Place in a container with a tightly fitting lid. Chill
before packing.
SERVES 1.

EXECUTIVE KEBAB

Serve with Italian pasta salad (page 45).

bite-sized pieces of: cooked chicken,
    sausage, ham, tongue, luncheon meat
    or roast lamb
apple chunks brushed with lemon juice
pineapple pieces
pickled onions or cocktail gherkins
chunks of cucumber, green pepper and
    cherry tomatoes
whole mushrooms

Thread bite-sized pieces of meat or poultry
alternately with vegetables, fruits and pickles
on small metal or wooden skewers. Place the
kebabs in a sealed container and chill before
packing. Pack a little mayonnaise or mustard
separately.

CHILLED POTATO AND LEEK SOUP

45 ml (3 tbsp) instant mashed potato
    powder
30 ml (2 tbsp) white onion soup powder
1 small piece carrot
1 leek, thinly sliced
1 small piece celery
300 ml (½ pint) boiling chicken stock
90 ml (6 tbsp) soured cream
60 ml (4 tbsp) dry white wine
salt and pepper to taste
a little extra stock

Place potato powder, soup powder, carrot,
leek and celery in an electric blender. Add
boiling stock and process until smooth. Add
soured cream and wine and blend again. Season with salt and pepper and chill. Thin down
with a little cold stock if desired. Pour into wide-
mouthed thermos and seal.
SERVES 2.

AUBERGINE PATE

*Serve pâté with fresh wholemeal bread and
follow with Five fruits salad (page 28).*

2 large aubergines
30 ml (2 tbsp) lemon juice
salt and black pepper to taste
45 ml (3 tbsp) oil
pinch garlic powder or dash juice

Wipe aubergines and place in baking tin.
Bake at 200 °C (400 °F, gas 6) for 30–40
minutes, turning occasionally. The aubergines
will be very soft when cooked. Allow them to
cool until they can be handled. Cut in half
lengthwise and scoop out soft flesh. Place
flesh in a blender or food processor, add
lemon juice and salt and pepper. Process until
smooth. Then, with machine running, slowly
add oil and process until blended. Mix in garlic
powder or juice. Spoon into containers and
chill, covered, for up to 6 days. Pack a small
knife with the lunch to spread pâté on buttered
wholemeal bread.
SERVES 4.

SALMON WINE SPREAD

*A light salmon spread to eat with dark rye
bread and a salad.*

60 ml (4 tbsp) dry white wine
1 bay leaf
10 peppercorns
pinch cayenne pepper
1 spring onion, chopped
15 ml (1 tbsp) lemon juice
2.5 ml (½ tsp) tomato paste
225 g (8 oz) canned salmon, drained
5 ml (1 tsp) chopped chives
60 ml (4 tbsp) natural yoghurt
60 ml (4 tbsp) soured cream
salt and lemon pepper to taste

Combine wine, bay leaf, peppercorns, cayenne pepper, spring onion and lemon juice in
a small saucepan and bring to the boil. Simmer until liquid is reduced by about a third,
then allow to cool. Strain, reserving liquid. Mix
reserved liquid with tomato paste. Flake salmon
and place in a blender or food processor. Add
reserved liquid, chives, yoghurt and half the
soured cream. Process until smooth. Beat in a
little more cream until desired consistency is
reached. Season with salt and lemon pepper.
Spoon into a dish or four individual serving
dishes and chill. Pack into the lunch box with
a wedge of lemon and slices of dark rye bread
or savoury biscuits.
SERVES 4.

POTTED CHEESE SPREAD

90 g (3 oz) butter, softened
225 g (8 oz) blue cheese, crumbled
125 ml (4 fl oz) fromage frais
45 ml (3 tbsp) port

Beat the butter, cheese and fromage frais until
well mixed. Gradually beat in port. Spoon
mixture into a serving dish and chill, covered,
until ready to pack. Pack a small portion of the
spread with savoury biscuits or pumpernickel.
If covered, the mixture will keep well in the
refrigerator for up to 10 days.
MAKES ABOUT 450 G (1 LB).

FIVE FRUITS SALAD

175 g (6 oz) fresh pineapple, cut into
    chunks
175 g (6 oz) peach slices
¼ honeydew melon, peeled, seeded and
    diced
90 g (3 oz) seedless green grapes
90 g (3 oz) fresh strawberries, halved

DRESSING
125 ml (4 fl oz) pineapple juice
30 ml (2 tbsp) orange liqueur

Combine fruits and toss lightly to mix. Combine pineapple juice and orange liqueur and
pour over fruits. Chill overnight, then pack.
Place in wide-mouthed thermos to keep cool if
desired. The fruit salad keeps, covered, in the
refrigerator for up to 3 days.
SERVES 4.

FRUIT TRIFLE

2 ginger biscuits, crushed
30 ml (2 tbsp) medium sherry
125 g (4 oz) canned fruit cocktail,
    drained
90 ml (6 tbsp) ready-made custard

Place crushed biscuits in the bottom of a small
container with a tightly fitting lid. Sprinkle with
half the sherry. Add remaining sherry to the
fruit cocktail and spoon into the container. Top
with the custard, seal well and chill before
packing.
SERVES 1.

*Clockwise from left: Italian pasta salad, Stuffed
tomatoes and Executive kebabs*

BOARDROOM LUNCHES

Business lunches are often working lunches. Meetings may be planned for lunch time but, instead of adjourning to the nearest restaurant, one can enjoy a light lunch at the office and business matters can be discussed in the privacy of the boardroom.

Many smaller businesses lack sophisticated kitchen facilities but, with careful planning, satisfying tasty meals can be prepared for lunch-hour meetings. The food preparation area does not need to be large, but it should have running water, refrigeration facilities and food preparation equipment such as kitchen knives, mixing bowls and cutting boards. Cooking should be kept to the minimum, so an electric frying pan and a small convection or microwave oven should be sufficient. A storage area is needed for crockery, cutlery, glassware, napkins, salad bowls, serving platters and utensils.

Even if you have only the basics in food preparation equipment and storage space, it is possible to prepare interesting and attractive lunches for small numbers of people. Perhaps the best choice for a boardroom lunch is one that is simple and light, with the emphasis on protein- and vitamin-rich foods. Nobody wants to eat a heavy, rich meal in the middle of the day, especially if there is a working afternoon ahead. Soups, open sandwiches and main-dish salads are quick to prepare and simple help-yourself meals such as antipasto and Danish sandwiches allow you to cater for individual tastes and are easy to serve and to eat.

BOARDROOM LUNCH MENUS

Prawn salad in lettuce cups
   (page 31)
Wheatgerm muffins (page 21)
Fruit trifle (page 28)

Baked potatoes (page 32)
Beef consommé, hot or cold, with
   soured cream
Cheese and fruit tray

Baked potatoes (page 32)
Cold meats
Vegetable salad

Smoked salmon sandwiches
   (page 32)
Gherkins, olives, tomato wedges
Fresh fruit salad (page 32)

Cold roast beef with mustard on
   French bread
Dill and cucumber salad (this page)
Fromage frais chive dip (this page)
   with fresh vegetables

Roquefort steak sandwiches
   (page 32)
Sliced tomatoes with Italian
   dressing (see Italian pasta salad,
   page 45)
Fresh fruit or cheese platter

Chicken and potato salad (page 31)
   with avocado and peaches,
   served with Wholemeal bread
   (page 18)

Antipasto as a whole meal (page 32)

Toasted sandwiches (page 31)
Crisp vegetable platter with Yoghurt
   dill dip (page 10)
Fresh fruit

Danish open sandwiches (page 31)
Marinated vegetables (page 46)
Fresh fruit

FROMAGE FRAIS CHIVE DIP

250 ml (8 fl oz) fromage frais
a little milk
15 ml (1 tbsp) lemon juice
5–6 radishes, finely chopped
10 ml (2 tsp) finely chopped chives
salt and pepper to taste
fresh vegetables, such as carrot and
   celery sticks, cauliflower florets and
   spring onions

Soften fromage frais with a little milk and the lemon juice. Stir in radishes and chives and season to taste with salt and pepper. Chill until needed. Place in a small serving bowl and surround with fresh vegetables.
MAKES ABOUT 300 ML (½ PINT).

DILL AND CUCUMBER SALAD

1 cucumber
275 g (10 oz) canned button mushrooms
100 ml (7 tbsp) white vinegar
25 ml (5 tsp) lemon juice
30 ml (2 tbsp) finely chopped fresh dill
   or 10 ml (2 tsp) dried
salt and black pepper to taste

Peel cucumber and slice thinly. Place in a small bowl and add drained mushrooms. Combine remaining ingredients and pour over cucumber and mushrooms. Chill several hours, or overnight.
SERVES 4.

PRAWN SALAD IN LETTUCE CUPS

Serve chilled with a wedge of lemon.

500 g (18 oz) small cooked prawns, shelled
60 ml (4 tbsp) fresh lemon juice
4 large lettuce leaves
lemon wedges

DRESSING
250 ml (8 fl oz) natural yoghurt
4 spring onions, thinly sliced
60 g (2 oz) cucumber, peeled, seeded and diced
30 ml (2 tbsp) lemon juice
2.5 ml (½ tsp) soy sauce
2.5 ml (½ tsp) dried dill
pepper to taste

Sprinkle the prawns with lemon juice and heap on lettuce leaves arranged on four plates. Garnish with lemon. To make dressing, mix yoghurt with onion and cucumber. Add remaining ingredients and season with pepper to taste. Spoon over prawns and serve immediately.
SERVES 4.

CHICKEN AND POTATO SALAD

Served with peach and avocado, this salad makes a complete meal.

1 cooked chicken
400 g (14 oz) canned new potatoes
30 ml (2 tbsp) chopped onion
1 small green pepper, seeded and chopped
200 ml (7 fl oz) mayonnaise
a little milk
salt and white pepper to taste
2 ripe peaches
1 large avocado
10 ml (2 tsp) lemon juice
lettuce leaves

Remove skin from chicken and cut flesh into bite-sized pieces. Drain potatoes and cut into bite-sized pieces. Combine chicken, potatoes, onion and green pepper in a mixing bowl. Thin mayonnaise with a little milk and add to bowl. Toss lightly to mix and season with salt and pepper to taste. Peel and remove stones from peaches and avocado. Cut into thin slices and sprinkle with lemon juice. Arrange fruit slices on one side of a serving platter. Line remaining side with lettuce leaves and mount potato chicken salad on them.
SERVES 4.

DANISH OPEN SANDWICHES

Open sandwiches can provide a delicious protein-rich lunch. Arrange ingredients attractively on platters and provide wholemeal or rye bread, pumpernickel, large crisp biscuits or crispbreads. Each person can make up his own lunch. Here are some ideas:

Lettuce leaves
Drained and flaked canned salmon
Rare roast beef, thinly sliced
Cucumber slices
Tomato slices
Prepared mustards
Mayonnaise
Shelled, deveined, cooked shrimps or prawns
Asparagus spears
Sliced, cooked chicken or turkey
Slices or wedges of cheese
Slices of hard-boiled egg
Cooked ham, thinly sliced
Smoked salmon
Liver pâté
Slices of pickles or gherkins

Toasted ham and cheese – just one of many flavour combinations

TOASTED SANDWICHES

Toasted sandwiches for a boardroom lunch should not be the soggy, greasy, corner café variety! Electric toasted sandwich makers are a joy to use and make it easy to serve a wide variety of crisp, hot sandwiches. Those that hold up to four double sandwiches at once are particularly useful. Refer to 'The Great Sandwich' (pages 11–16) for sandwich ideas. Many of the fillings given in that chapter can be used in toasted sandwiches too – ham, egg or chicken salad, tuna salad, cottage cheese fillings and cheese fillings.

Other filling ideas:
☆ chopped pickle and chopped ham with grated cheese of your choice
☆ chopped ham or other cooked meat, sliced tomato and garlic salt
☆ grated cheese of your choice, prawns, a little white sauce, dash lemon juice, salt and pepper
☆ chopped hard-boiled egg mixed with cream cheese, tomato slices, salt and pepper

☆ cooked minced beef mixed with egg yolk, herbs, salt, pepper, a little mustard and tomato sauce

☆ layers of sliced tomato, grated Parmesan cheese, anchovy fillets and sliced stuffed olives

☆ thin slices of roast pork, a little apple sauce and a sprinkling of dried sage

☆ liver pâté with sliced tomatoes and chopped spring onions

☆ liver pâté with sliced gherkins and crumbled blue cheese

☆ cooked white fish, flaked and mixed with lemon juice, mayonnaise and chopped capers

☆ cottage cheese, sliced tomato, chopped chives

☆ drained flaked salmon mixed with mayonnaise, lemon juice, chopped hard-boiled eggs, a few chopped capers and fresh dill

ROQUEFORT STEAK SANDWICHES

These delicious hot sandwiches can be prepared almost anywhere as the only cooking item needed is an electric frying pan.

125 g (4 oz) Roquefort or other blue cheese
100 g (3½ oz) butter, softened
few drops Worcestershire sauce
10 ml (2 tsp) chopped fresh parsley
8 tender, boneless steaks, about 1 cm (½ inch) thick
coarsely ground black pepper
4 slices rye bread, lightly buttered

Grate or crumble the cheese and mix with 75 g (2½ oz) of the butter to form a smooth paste. Mix in Worcestershire sauce and parsley. Heat remaining butter in an electric frying pan and sauté steaks over high heat for about 2 minutes on each side. Season with pepper. Lower heat and spoon butter mixture over steaks. Cover pan with lid and leave just long enough to melt butter. Serve steaks immediately on buttered rye bread.
SERVES 4.

SMOKED SALMON SANDWICHES

4 slices rye bread, toasted and buttered
12 slices smoked salmon
fresh dill
4 lemon wedges
4 spring onions, finely chopped
60 ml (4 tbsp) drained capers
black pepper

Arrange 3 slices of salmon on each piece of bread and garnish with fresh dill. Add a lemon wedge, some chopped onion and capers to each plate. Serve sprinkled with black pepper, and accompanied by gherkins, olives and tomato wedges.
SERVES 4.

BAKED POTATOES

Potatoes baked in a portable convection or microwave oven provide the base for a tasty hot meal. Serve with a variety of toppings and a green salad.

1 large potato per person
30 g (1 oz) butter per potato
milk
salt and pepper

Wash potato, then prick it with a fork. Bake at 190 °C (375 °F, gas 5) for about 1 hour in a convection oven, or about 6 minutes in a microwave oven. Cut a cross in top of potato and gently squeeze base to open. Scoop out potato flesh and mash with half the butter, a little milk and seasoning. Pile flesh back into shell and top with remaining butter, or add any of the following flavourings. Reheat if necessary.

VARIATIONS

Cheesy potatoes For each potato, grate 60 g (2 oz) Cheddar cheese and add most of it to the mash. Stir in 2.5 ml (½ tsp) prepared mustard and 30 ml (2 tbsp) chopped cooked ham, or 1 rasher bacon, cooked and crumbled. Pile flesh back in potato skin, top with remaining cheese and heat through.
Corned beef potatoes For each potato, add 60 g (2 oz) chopped corned beef and 10 ml (2 tsp) tomato ketchup to the mash. Pile into skin and heat through. Top with a little soured cream and chopped fresh parsley.
Soured cream potatoes For each potato, add 30 ml (2 tbsp) soured cream, 30 ml (2 tbsp) crumbled blue cheese and 2.5 ml (½ tsp) chopped chives to the mash. Pile in skin and heat through. Sprinkle with a few chopped chives.
Vegetable stuffed potatoes Into the mashed flesh of each potato, stir some grated cheese of your choice, cooked peas, chopped cooked carrots, a little finely diced green pepper and a little chopped spring onion. Season with salt and pepper and add enough cream to make a soft mixture. Spoon into potato shells and heat through. Top with a little grated cheese and serve with cold meats.

Meaty baked potatoes For 4 potatoes, scoop out flesh of baked potatoes and add 200 g (7 oz) chopped cooked meat. Add 15 ml (1 tbsp) chopped fresh parsley, 15 ml (1 tbsp) chopped spring onion, celery salt and pepper to taste, 30 ml (2 tbsp) butter and enough cream to make a soft mixture. Spoon into potato skins and heat through.

ANTIPASTO

A selection of ingredients arranged attractively makes an interesting and easy-to-prepare lunch. Choose as many or as few items from the following list as you wish, remembering to contrast flavours and colours. Let everyone make their own choice from the platter.

Anchovies
Sardines
Tuna
Red and green peppers
Pickled artichokes
Sliced prosciutto
Sliced salami
Pasta salad
Celery sticks
Mushroom salad
Olives
Lettuce
Tomatoes
Radishes
Spring onions
Ricotta cheese
Stuffed or devilled eggs
Melon, peeled and sliced
Breadsticks

FRESH FRUIT SALAD

2 ripe pears, peeled, cored and diced
1 large apple, peeled and sliced
1 grapefruit, peeled and divided into segments
1 banana, peeled and sliced
1 small melon, cut into cubes, or use a melon baller
175 g (6 oz) seedless grapes, halved
a few strawberries, halved
a few lychees, hulled and seeded
45 g (1½ oz) caster sugar
30 ml (2 tbsp) Kirsch or other fruit liqueur

Place all fruits in a bowl. Sprinkle with sugar and liqueur and toss to mix. Cover and chill for a few hours, or overnight. Serve with fresh cream.
SERVES 4.

Help yourself to Antipasto

GREAT SNACKS

When we look for something to nibble, we think too often of commercially prepared snacks. These foods – including sweets and chips or crisps – may supply a certain amount of instant energy but they are high in empty calories as they contain little in the way of nutrients. They are fatty or full of sugar . . . but they do taste good. It's difficult to understand that what tastes good may not necessarily be good for you, so it is quite a challenge to change the eating habits of the children and adults in your family to snack foods that have nutritive value. Healthy snacks can taste great and supply some of the important nutrients we need every day.

The delicious sweet and savoury snack foods for which recipes are given here will help you change your family's habits and they contain the healthiest ingredients: cheese, wholemeal flour, nuts, fresh and dried fruits, all of which pack a lot of punch into the lunch box in terms of energy and nutrients.

SAVOURY SESAME FINGERS

Good with Yoghurt dill dip (page 10).

125 g (4 oz) wholemeal flour
90 g (3 oz) mature Cheddar cheese,
   finely grated
pinch salt
pinch dry mustard
pinch cayenne pepper
75 ml (5 tbsp) oil
30 ml (2 tbsp) cold water
30 ml (2 tbsp) sesame seeds

Combine flour, cheese, salt, mustard and cayenne pepper in a bowl. Add oil and mix until crumbly. Add cold water gradually to form a soft dough. Roll dough between two pieces of waxed paper to a 38 × 30 cm (15 × 12 inch) rectangle. Remove top piece of waxed paper and place a greased and lightly floured baking sheet over dough. Invert so that dough is on the baking sheet, then remove second piece of waxed paper. Sprinkle with sesame seeds and press them in lightly with hands or rolling pin. Cut dough into fingers, bake at 190 °C (375 °F, gas 5) for 15 minutes, then remove to a wire rack to cool. When cool, place in a container with a tightly fitting lid. Pack a few sesame fingers in the lunch box for a savoury snack.

MAKES ABOUT 60 SESAME FINGERS.

TANGY CORN CHIPS

Great snacks, delicious with dips or a salad.

150 g (5 oz) cornmeal
90 ml (6 tbsp) wholemeal flour
2.5 ml (½ tsp) salt
2.5 ml (½ tsp) bicarbonate of soda
2.5 ml (½ tsp) chilli powder
125 ml (4 fl oz) buttermilk
45 ml (3 tbsp) oil
10 ml (2 tsp) coarse salt

Spread 75 g (2½ oz) cornmeal in a shallow baking tin and toast in the oven at 180 °C (350 °F, gas 4) for 15 minutes. Combine toasted cornmeal with remaining cornmeal, flour, salt, bicarbonate of soda and chilli powder. Mix buttermilk and oil and add to dry ingredients, stirring until dough forms a ball. Turn out on a floured surface and knead for about 5 minutes. Divide dough in half and roll each half into a 30 cm (12 inch) square. Sprinkle dough with coarse salt. Press salt in with a rolling pin. Cut into 2.5 cm (1 inch) squares and place on a lightly greased baking sheet. Bake at 180 °C (350 °F, gas 4) for about 15 minutes, or until lightly browned. Cool on baking sheet for 5 minutes, then transfer to a wire rack and cool completely. Store in a tightly covered container.

MAKES ABOUT 200 CHIPS.

SAVOURY GRANOLA SNACKS

Granola is usually sweetish, but here's a recipe with a herb and onion flavour.

175 g (6 oz) rolled oats
100 g (3½ oz) wholemeal flour
60 ml (4 tbsp) wheatgerm
60 ml (4 tbsp) sunflower seeds
15 ml (1 tbsp) clear honey
5 ml (1 tsp) onion salt
2.5 ml (½ tsp) dried marjoram
5 ml (1 tsp) dried thyme
pinch dried tarragon
60 g (2 oz) flaked almonds
3 eggs
200 ml (7 fl oz) oil

In a large mixing bowl, combine oats, flour, wheatgerm, seeds, honey, onion salt, herbs and almonds. Toss to mix. Beat eggs and oil together, then stir into oatmeal mixture until well blended. Spread mixture evenly in a greased Swiss roll tin and bake at 200 °C (400 °F, gas 6) for about 20 minutes, until light golden brown. Place tin on wire rack and cut granola into squares, then halve each square diagonally to form triangles. Cool in tin, then store in a tightly covered container in the refrigerator. These snacks are good by themselves, or with a dip.

MAKES ABOUT 72 GRANOLA SNACKS.

CHEESE AND HERB BISCUITS

Prepare the dough well ahead, and bake a few biscuits when needed.

125 g (4 oz) wholemeal flour
125 g (4 oz) Cheddar cheese, grated
2.5 ml (½ tsp) salt
good pinch onion salt
2.5 ml (½ tsp) crumbled dried sage
2.5 ml (½ tsp) dried mixed herbs
pinch cayenne pepper
60 ml (4 tbsp) oil
about 45 ml (3 tbsp) cold water

Combine flour, cheese, salt, onion salt, sage, mixed herbs and cayenne pepper in a bowl. Add oil and mix in. Add enough cold water to form a dough. Cover and chill for about 15 minutes, or until firm. At this stage, the dough may be kept in the refrigerator for several days. To bake, roll dough out on a lightly floured surface and cut into circles. Place biscuits on an ungreased baking sheet and prick each with a fork. Bake at 180 °C (350 °F, gas 4) for about 15 minutes, or until golden. Remove from baking sheet and cool on a wire rack. Store in a tightly covered container.
MAKES ABOUT 24 BISCUITS.

OLIVE BITES

Three or four of these cheesy olive bites will instantly banish hunger pangs.

125 g (4 oz) Cheddar cheese, grated
60 g (2 oz) butter, softened
2.5 ml (½ tsp) paprika
2.5 ml (½ tsp) dry mustard
pinch salt
90 g (3 oz) plain flour
24 stuffed green olives

Combine cheese, butter, paprika, mustard and salt, and mix well. Add flour and mix well to form a dough. Shape a little dough around each olive, covering it completely. Place on an ungreased baking sheet and bake at 200 °C (400 °F, gas 6) for 12–15 minutes, or until golden brown. Store in a tightly sealed container.
MAKES 24 BITES.

POPCORN

Popcorn tastes good, is low in calories and is a good source of fibre. Electric popcorn makers do the job more quickly and easily, but you can use a large covered saucepan on the stove. To pop popcorn without an electric machine, allow about 60 ml (4 tbsp) oil for 125 g (4 oz) unpopped popcorn. Place oil and popcorn in the saucepan and place over medium-high heat. When the first kernels start to pop, cover the saucepan. Shake pan over the heat until no more popping is heard, then transfer popped corn to a large bowl, and season as desired. Most popcorn expands during popping in a ratio of about 15 to 1, so a little goes a long way and it makes an inexpensive snack. You can store popped popcorn in a container with a tightly fitting lid for only 1–2 days, so it's best to make small quantities. Pack into sandwich bags, seal well and tuck into the lunch box for a special treat.

POPCORN SEASONINGS

Melted butter and salt are the classic seasonings for popcorn, but here are some interesting flavours to try. All seasonings are for the above amount of popcorn.
Curried popcorn Melt 30 g (1 oz) butter and pour over popped corn. Combine 5 ml (1 tsp) curry powder, 2.5 ml (½ tsp) each turmeric and ground ginger and a pinch of cayenne pepper. Sprinkle over popcorn. Add salt to taste and toss to coat.
Herb popcorn Melt 45 g (1½ oz) butter and pour over popcorn. Combine ½ chicken stock cube, 5 ml (1 tsp) dried (or 15 ml (1 tbsp) chopped fresh) parsley, 2.5 ml (1 tsp) dried sage, 2.5 ml (½ tsp) celery salt, 5 ml (1 tsp) dried marjoram, and sprinkle over corn. Toss to mix well.
Savoury popcorn Combine 1 small packet pretzel rings with the popcorn in a large baking tin. Melt 60 g (2 oz) butter over low heat and stir in 30 ml (2 tbsp) onion soup powder. Pour butter mixture over popcorn and pretzels and stir to coat evenly. Heat at 160 °C (325 °F, gas 3) for 10 minutes, stirring once. Cool, then store in a container with a tightly fitting lid.

PEANUTS AND POPCORN

60 g (2 oz) butter
150 g (5 oz) clear honey
150 g (5 oz) popped popcorn
150 g (5 oz) salted peanuts
2.5 ml (½ tsp) seasoning salt

Combine butter and honey in a saucepan. Heat, stirring, until butter has melted and mixture is well blended. Allow the mixture to cool. Meanwhile, mix popcorn and peanuts in a large bowl. Sprinkle with seasoning salt. Pour cooled butter mixture over popcorn and peanuts, tossing to coat well. Spread mixture on a lightly greased baking sheet, and bake at 180 °C (350 °F, gas 4) for 5–10 minutes. Watch carefully, as the mixture should be crisp but not browned. Allow the mixture to cool in the pan, then store peanuts and popcorn in a container with a tightly fitting lid. To pack, fill sandwich bags with the mixture and seal well.
SERVES 6.

NUTTY WHEAT SAVOURY

225 g (8 oz) butter or margarine
15 ml (1 tbsp) Worcestershire sauce
225 g (8 oz) bite-sized shredded wheat cereal
200 g (7 oz) walnuts, coarsely chopped
5 ml (1 tsp) salt

Melt butter or margarine in a large roasting tin. Stir in Worcestershire sauce, then add cereal and nuts, stirring to coat evenly. Bake in oven at 180 °C (350 °F, gas 4) for 20 minutes, stirring well two or three times. Sprinkle with salt. Cool, then place in a tightly covered container. Store in a cool place; the mixture will keep for at least 2 weeks.
SERVES 6–8.

VARIATION
Add a sprinkling of grated Parmesan cheese mixed with a little onion salt while the mixture is still warm.

MOLASSES SQUARES ❄

75 g (2½ oz) butter, softened
150 g (5 oz) clear honey
200 ml (7 fl oz) molasses
4 egg whites
125 g (4 oz) wholemeal flour
90 g (3 oz) plain flour
2.5 ml (½ tsp) bicarbonate of soda
pinch grated nutmeg
2.5 ml (½ tsp) salt
90 g (3 oz) desiccated coconut

Place butter, honey and molasses in a large mixing bowl and beat until smooth. An electric mixer works best. Beat in egg whites. Mix together flours, bicarbonate of soda, nutmeg, salt and coconut and add to butter mixture. Mix well, then spread in a greased Swiss roll tin. Bake at 180 °C (350 °F, gas 4) for about 30 minutes. Allow to cool in the tin for 5 minutes, then cut into 5 cm (2 inch) squares. Place squares between sheets of waxed paper and store in a container with a tightly fitting lid.
MAKES ABOUT 35 SQUARES.

APPLE TURNOVERS ❅

A sweet snack that freezes well.

500 g (18 oz) apples, peeled, cored and
  sliced
60 ml (4 tbsp) water
60 g (2 oz) caster sugar
45 g (1½ oz) ground almonds
45 g (1½ oz) currants
2.5 ml (½ tsp) ground cinnamon
400 g (14 oz) frozen puff pastry, thawed
beaten egg for glazing

Place apples in a saucepan, add water and
simmer gently for about 5 minutes, or until
apples are just soft. Drain, then add sugar,
almonds, currants and cinnamon to apples,
mixing well. Roll out pastry to a 30 × 40 cm (12
× 16 inch) rectangle and cut into 10 cm (4 inch)
squares. Spoon apple filling onto each square,
then dampen edges and fold pastry over. Seal
edges with a fork. Place turnovers on a damp-
ened baking sheet and brush with beaten egg.
Bake at 200 °C (400 °F, gas 6) for 20–25
minutes, or until golden brown and well puffed.
Cool on a wire rack. To freeze, open-freeze,
then place in a rigid container. Seal well.
MAKES 12 TURNOVERS.

APPLE SAUCE SQUARES ❅

*A delicious snack – good with a cup of coffee
and great with a glass of cold milk.*

375 ml (13 fl oz) apple sauce
150 g (5 oz) butter or margarine, melted
200 g (7 oz) caster sugar
125 g (4 oz) plain flour
125 g (4 oz) wholemeal flour
10 ml (2 tsp) bicarbonate of soda
5 ml (1 tsp) ground cinnamon
150 g (5 oz) sultanas
30 ml (2 tbsp) wheatgerm

Heat apple sauce to simmering. Pour into a
large mixing bowl and add melted butter and
sugar. Stir well. Sift flours, bicarbonate of soda
and cinnamon together and add to apple sauce
mixture. Add sultanas and wheatgerm, mixing
well. Spoon mixture into two greased 20 cm (8
inch) square baking tins and bake at 190 °C
(375 °F, gas 5) for 25–30 minutes, until a
skewer inserted in the centre comes out clean.
Cool in tin on wire rack, then cut into squares.
Sprinkle with icing sugar if desired. Store well
covered, or freeze.
MAKES ABOUT 24 SQUARES.

HOME-MADE CRUNCHY GRANOLA

*It tastes so good, you'll never guess that it's
good for you too! For variety, try adding other
kinds of nuts and dried fruit.*

175 g (6 oz) rolled oats
60 g (2 oz) desiccated coconut
90 g (3 oz) wheatgerm
100 g (3½ oz) flaked almonds
45 ml (3 tbsp) soft brown sugar
60 ml (4 tbsp) sesame seeds
60 ml (4 tbsp) sunflower seeds
2.5 ml (½ tsp) grated nutmeg
pinch ground cloves
5 ml (1 tsp) ground cinnamon
150 g (5 oz) clear honey
125 ml (4 fl oz) oil
75 g (2½ oz) dried apricots, coarsely
  chopped

In a large mixing bowl combine oats, coconut,
wheatgerm, almonds, brown sugar, seeds
and spices. Toss to mix. Combine honey and
oil and pour over oat mixture, stirring until
all ingredients are well mixed. Spoon mixture
into a large heavy frying pan and heat,
stirring constantly, for about 5 minutes, or
until oats turn golden brown. Remove from
heat and stir in apricots. Allow mixture to
cool, then store in a container with a tightly
fitting lid.
SERVES 8.

RUSKS

Just the thing for tea break.

1.25 kg (2½ lb) plain flour
45 ml (3 tbsp) bicarbonate of soda
30 ml (2 tbsp) cream of tartar
7.5 ml (1½ tsp) salt
400 g (14 oz) caster sugar
5 ml (1 tsp) crushed aniseed
500 g (18 oz) butter or margarine
2 eggs, beaten
625 ml (21 fl oz) buttermilk

Sift flour with bicarbonate of soda, cream of
tartar and salt into a large mixing bowl. Add
sugar and aniseed, then rub in butter or margarine. Mix beaten eggs and buttermilk and
stir into dry ingredients to make a soft dough.
Form dough into balls and place in greased
loaf tins. Bake at 180 °C (350 °F, gas 4) for 35–
45 minutes. Turn out and cool on wire rack,
then break apart. Dry rusks in a slow oven
(110 °C, 225 °F, gas 2) until crisp but not too
brown. Store in airtight containers.
MAKES ABOUT 84 RUSKS (RECIPE CAN BE
HALVED).

RAISIN NUGGETS ❅

175 g (6 oz) butter or margarine,
  softened
200 g (7 oz) soft brown sugar
2 eggs
175 g (6 oz) plain flour
10 ml (2 tsp) baking powder
5 ml (1 tsp) ground cinnamon
good pinch grated nutmeg
2.5 ml (½ tsp) salt
125 g (4 oz) walnuts or hazelnuts,
  chopped
150 g (5 oz) seedless raisins

Beat butter and sugar until fluffy. Beat in eggs,
one at a time, mixing well after each addition.
Sift flour, baking powder, cinnamon, nutmeg
and salt together and stir into egg mixture with
nuts and raisins. Mix well, then drop spoonfuls
onto a greased baking sheet. Bake at 180 °C
(350 °F, gas 4) for 10–12 minutes, or until
lightly browned. Remove to a wire rack to
cool. Store in a tightly covered container or
freeze.
MAKES ABOUT 48 NUGGETS.

CRISPY CINNAMON ROUNDS ❅

75 ml (5 tbsp) oil
75 ml (5 tbsp) golden syrup
few drops caramel essence
75 ml (5 tbsp) natural yoghurt
75 g (2½ oz) wholemeal flour
5 ml (1 tsp) bicarbonate of soda
pinch salt
5 ml (1 tsp) ground cinnamon

Combine oil, syrup, flavouring and yoghurt in
a bowl and beat until smooth. Mix flour, bicarbonate of soda, salt and cinnamon and add to
yoghurt mixture. Stir until well blended, then
drop by small spoonfuls onto a greased and
floured baking sheet. Leave about 5 cm (2
inches) between each round. Bake at 180 °C
(350 °F, gas 4) for 10 minutes, then remove
from oven and stand on baking sheet for about
3 minutes. Remove rounds to a wire rack to
cool. When cool, place rounds between layers
of waxed paper and store in a container with a
tightly fitting lid.
MAKES ABOUT 48 ROUNDS.

FRUIT AND VEGETABLES

*Remember that fruit and vegetables aren't
limited to mealtimes – they make great snacks
too. They are crisp and juicy, full of vitamins
and minerals and taste terrific. Sliced fruits
and vegetables must be packed in plastic bags
or sealed containers. Most of them taste good*

with a yoghurt or fromage frais dip. Some vegetables, such as courgettes and button mushrooms and some fruits, such as sliced apple, banana or peaches, should be brushed lightly with lemon juice to prevent discoloration. Here's a list of fruit and vegetable snacks:

FRUITS
Apple, whole or cut into wedges
Pear
Plums
Tangerines
Orange
Pineapple rings
Fresh strawberries
Banana
A small container of fruit salad
A small container of melon balls
Bunch of grapes

Fresh lychees
Kiwi fruit slices
Grapefruit segments
Fresh peach
Fresh apricots
Watermelon

VEGETABLES
Celery sticks
Carrot sticks
Cucumber slices
Fresh, whole green beans
Cauliflower florets
Broccoli florets
Green pepper strips
Fennel slices
Courgette wedges
Radishes

Cherry tomatoes
Whole button mushrooms
Alfalfa sprouts

OTHER SNACK IDEAS
Fried chicken wings
Miniature meatballs
Quarters of hard-boiled egg
Breadsticks, broken into short lengths
Pretzels
Melba toast
Crispbreads or wafers
A container of natural yoghurt with fruit slices
A piece of cheese with two biscuits
Cooked sausage

Clockwise from left: Home-made crunchy granola, Crispy cinnamon rounds and Rusks

SLIMMERS' LUNCHES

Dieting is probably a more popular topic of debate than any other, including the national debt, the state of the economy and the latest sport tour. It is discussed at cocktail parties while everyone shovels down fattening titbits and sips glasses of wine. It is a favourite topic at tea break, over tea with sugar and sticky buns and it is sure to come up at dinner parties, usually when dessert is served. Thousands of pounds are spent annually on diet aids and hundreds of diets promising instant and incredible weight loss appear. But let's face it – there is no magical cure. The bottom line is that losing weight means eating less.

The only way to rid your self of excess pounds and keep them off is to cut down on your calorie intake. An increase in exercise will help burn up calories and the best exercise for slimmers is pushing away from the table. Sticking to a diet at the office, in the classroom or anywhere outside your own home is not easy. The temptation to eat sweets and junk foods and to drink sugary canned drinks is always there and you will have to strengthen your determination and will-power and learn to say 'no'. Packed lunches for slimmers do take time to plan and some extra effort to prepare, but it is well worth it. Be sure to plan well-balanced meals consisting of small helpings of a wide variety of foods, including servings from all the food groups to help you maintain good health. Do not skip meals. If you think you can go without lunch at the office, you may spend an uncomfortable afternoon with decreased productivity just because you are hungry. And, on top of that, you are very likely to overeat at dinner to make up for it.

The menu suggestions given here are all for packable lunches which you can take anywhere. Some can be made ahead; some are assembled in the morning, before you leave for work. Each menu contains about 285 calories, or approximately one-third of the calories you need daily if you want to reduce. Each lunch is light, satisfying and contains a good amount of the day's requirements of nutrients. The menus can help you control your calorie intake if you plan your other meals around them. With a little practice and a good calorie chart you will be able to mix and match soups, salads and sandwiches, even be able to add some desserts to your menus and still keep your packed lunches on the slimming side.

NOTE: 1 calorie equals 4.2 kilojoules.

SLIMMING HINTS

☆ Never skip a meal, especially not breakfast. Learn to eat small meals, more frequently if necessary.

☆ When you get up in the morning, drink at least one glass of mineral water. It tastes good and is good for you. Drink a glass of water before meals to help curb your appetite and continue to sip water throughout the day.

☆ Keep a record of all the foods you eat – even those 'tastes' as you are cooking. You will be surprised to see how much you actually do eat and you can easily see where to cut down.

☆ Never eat while you are doing something else, such as reading or watching TV. It's easy to consume too much food if you are not concentrating on what you eat.

☆ To keep down the calorie count on salads, use lemon juice or a flavoured vinegar, such as tarragon, instead of salad dressing or mayonnaise. For added flavour,

MENUS FOR SLIMMERS' LUNCHES

Fromage frais peach salad (page 39)
Celery sticks and dill pickle

Open salmon sandwich (page 41)
Cucumber and yoghurt salad (page 39) served with Wholemeal bread (page 18)
1 medium apple

Cottage cheese surprise sandwich (page 42)
Celery and carrot sticks
Minty pineapple (page 42)
1 Coconut meringue (page 42

Mushroom salad (page 40)
1 slice brown bread
1 pear

Beef stroganoff (page 41)
Orange and banana fruit salad (page 42)

Cream of vegetable soup with lemon (page 40)
1 crispbread
1 apple

Tomato yoghurt soup (page 40)
Orange and carrot salad (page 39)
1 crispbread
Baked pear (page 42)

---

1 Scotch egg (page 39)
Bean salad (page 40)
1 Coconut meringue (page 42)

Tomatoes with chicken salad stuffing (page 39)
1 crispbread
A small bunch grapes

Hearty vegetable soup (page 40)
Slimmers' tuna salad (page 40)
2 plums
1 Crunchy oat biscuit (page 42)

sprinkle grated citrus rind over vegetables, salads and fruits. A little grated cheese adds flavour to vegetables and salads.

☆ If you are using canned fruits or seafood, look for those that are packed in natural juice or water rather than in heavy syrup or oil.

☆ Add a bit of soy sauce or a splash of wine to meat instead of thick gravy. Try sprinkling ground spices on desserts and fruits instead of using rich toppings.

☆ Remember, the presentation of food influences how you feel about eating. Make open sandwiches and arrange ingredients attractively. Cut sandwiches into quarters or smaller pieces so slimmers will feel they are eating more.

☆ You can carry hot broth or consommé in a thermos flask, or keep soup powder or stock cubes in your desk drawer and make them up with boiling water at lunch time.

☆ Cut down on alcohol intake. Wines, beer and liqueurs are high in calories but very low in nutrients.

☆ Cut down on sugary foods and on sugar in beverages. Use artificial sweeteners or, better still, drink unsweetened tea and coffee. Drink diet canned drinks.

☆ Use skimmed milk instead of whole milk for drinking and cooking.

☆ You can stay on your diet when eating out. Look for foods low in calories – such as salads and vegetable dishes – and go for grilled meat and fish.

☆ Remember to trim fats from meat and skin from poultry before cooking. This will reduce the calorie count. Don't eat dishes with heavy sauces or sauces made with cream or with rich, cheesy toppings.

☆ To deal with mid-morning hunger pangs, when friends are eating sweets, buns and toasted sandwiches, keep a supply of crisp celery or carrot sticks in a plastic bag to nibble on.

☆ Learn to say 'no' when friends press second helpings on you, or invite you to share sweets, cakes and other fattening foods.

SCOTCH EGGS

1 hard-boiled egg
a little plain flour
60 g (2 oz) raw sausagemeat
good pinch dried mixed herbs
5 ml (1 tsp) finely chopped onion
a little pepper
30 ml (2 tbsp) dried breadcrumbs
hot oil for frying

Peel egg and dip in flour, coating well. Mix sausagemeat with herbs, onion and a little pepper. Press meat mixture around egg, covering completely. Roll in breadcrumbs, then deep-fry in hot oil for about 3 minutes, or until golden brown. Drain and chill.
SERVES 1. (181 CALORIES.)

TOMATOES WITH CHICKEN SALAD STUFFING

3 large tomatoes
2.5 ml (½ tsp) garlic salt
½ small onion, chopped
½ stick celery, chopped
5 ml (1 tsp) chopped green pepper
200 g (7 oz) cooked chicken, chopped
5 ml (1 tsp) lemon juice
5 ml (1 tsp) chopped fresh parsley
10 ml (2 tsp) French dressing
pepper to taste

Cut tops from tomatoes and scoop out pulp. Chop pulp, then drain well. Sprinkle inside of tomatoes with garlic salt. Combine tomato pulp, onion, celery, green pepper, cooked chicken, lemon juice, chopped parsley and French dressing. Season to taste with pepper. Spoon mixture into tomato shells and replace tops. Wrap well or place in plastic containers and seal well. Chill before packing.
SERVES 3. (118 CALORIES A PORTION.)

ORANGE AND CARROT SALAD

250 g (9 oz) carrots, peeled and sliced
juice of ½ orange
45 ml (3 tbsp) Slimmers' salad dressing (this page)
15 ml (1 tbsp) chopped onion
10 ml (2 tsp) chopped fresh parsley
2.5 ml (½ tsp) grated orange rind
salt to taste
lettuce leaves

Cook carrots in boiling salted water until just tender – about 8 minutes. Drain well, then add orange juice. Mix salad dressing with onion, parsley and orange rind and season to taste with salt. Pour over carrots and toss to coat. Chill well. To pack, line a container with lettuce leaves and add one-third of the salad. Seal container and place in lunch box.
SERVES 3. (57 CALORIES A PORTION.)

> NOTE: This salad keeps well in the refrigerator for several days.

SLIMMERS' SALAD DRESSING

100 ml (7 tbsp) cider vinegar
25 ml (5 tsp) lemon juice
15 ml (1 tbsp) tomato ketchup
15 ml (1 tbsp) Worcestershire sauce
10 ml (2 tsp) soy sauce
1 clove garlic, minced
2.5 ml (½ tsp) dry mustard
good pinch paprika
salt and pepper to taste
liquid artificial sweetener to taste

Place all ingredients in a jar with a tightly fitting lid and shake well. Use as required.
MAKES ABOUT 150 ML (¼ PINT). (EVERY 15 ML (1 TBSP) DRESSING CONTAINS ABOUT 39 CALORIES.)

FROMAGE FRAIS PEACH SALAD

400 g (14 oz) peach halves, drained
250 ml (8 fl oz) fromage frais
15 ml (1 tbsp) sultanas
2.5 ml (½ tsp) chopped chives
15 ml (1 tbsp) chopped fresh parsley
2.5 ml (½ tsp) salt

Rinse drained peach halves in cold water, then drain again. Set 4 peach halves aside and chop remainder. Mix with remaining ingredients. Place 2 reserved peach halves in a plastic container and pile half the fromage frais mixture on top. Repeat with remaining peach halves and fromage frais. Chill before packing in lunch box.
SERVES 2. (248 CALORIES A PORTION.)

CUCUMBER AND YOGHURT SALAD

1 large cucumber, unpeeled, thinly sliced
1 small onion, thinly sliced
10 ml (2 tsp) chopped fresh mint
125 ml (4 fl oz) low-fat natural yoghurt
5 ml (1 tsp) lemon juice
onion salt and pepper to taste

Place cucumber slices in a mixing bowl. Add onion and mint. Mix yoghurt with lemon juice, onion salt and pepper and pour over cucumber. Mix so that cucumber slices are coated. Chill well in the refrigerator. To serve, place half of the salad in a plastic container and seal well.
SERVES 2. (31 CALORIES A PORTION.)

> NOTE: This salad keeps well in the refrigerator for up to 3 days.

SLIMMERS' TUNA SALAD

45 ml (3 tbsp) wine vinegar
2.5 ml (½ tsp) caster sugar
2.5 ml (½ tsp) dried basil
pinch pepper
5 ml (1 tsp) lemon juice
200 g (7 oz) canned tuna in brine,
    drained and flaked
4 small tomatoes, peeled and cut into
    wedges
45 ml (3 tbsp) chopped onion
½ medium cucumber, sliced
½ stick celery, chopped
shredded lettuce to serve (⅛ head for
    each person)

Mix vinegar, sugar, basil, pepper and lemon juice. Chill. Combine tuna, tomato wedges, onion, cucumber slices and celery. Add vinegar mixture and toss to coat evenly. Chill well. To pack, place a quarter of tuna mixture in a plastic container, top with shredded lettuce, seal well, and add to each lunch. At lunch time, mix lettuce into tuna mixture.
SERVES 4. (74 CALORIES A PORTION.)

MUSHROOM SALAD

300 g (11 oz) button mushrooms,
    halved
125 g (4 oz) cooked ham, chopped
¼ small cucumber, diced
1 spring onion, chopped
150 ml (¼ pint) low-fat natural yoghurt
2.5 ml (½ tsp) curry powder
10 ml (2 tsp) lemon juice
salt and pepper to taste
30 ml (2 tbsp) chutney

Combine mushrooms, ham, cucumber and onion in a bowl. Mix yoghurt with curry powder, lemon juice, salt, pepper and chutney. Add yoghurt mixture to mushrooms. Stir well. Chill, then pack into lunch boxes.
SERVES 4. (71 CALORIES A PORTION.)

BEAN SALAD

400 g (14 oz) canned butter beans,
    drained
300 g (11 oz) mushrooms, sliced
4 spring onions, sliced
150 ml (¼ pint) low-fat natural yoghurt
salt and pepper to taste

Combine beans, mushrooms and onions with yoghurt and season with salt and pepper. Chill well, then pack into plastic containers with lids for packed lunches.
SERVES 4. (48 CALORIES A PORTION.)

TUNA AND FRUIT SALAD

1 medium apple, unpeeled, cored
½ medium lettuce, shredded
100 g (3½ oz) canned tuna in brine,
    drained and flaked
90 g (3 oz) seedless grapes
30 ml (2 tbsp) mayonnaise
60 ml (4 tbsp) Slimmers' salad dressing
    (page 39)

Cut apple into cubes and mix with lettuce, tuna and grapes. Cover and chill well. Mix mayonnaise and Slimmers' salad dressing together. Pack apple mixture into two containers and seal well. Pack mayonnaise mixture in separate containers and add to lunch box. At lunch time, pour mayonnaise over salad.
SERVES 2. (219 CALORIES A PORTION.)

ASPARAGUS VINAIGRETTE

450 g (1 lb) canned asparagus spears,
    drained
90 ml (6 tbsp) Slimmers' salad dressing
    (page 39)
30 ml (2 tbsp) dry white wine
30 ml (2 tbsp) finely chopped onion
30 ml (2 tbsp) chopped green pepper
15 ml (1 tbsp) chopped fresh parsley
15 ml (1 tbsp) finely chopped gherkin
2 small tomatoes, sliced

Place asparagus spears in one layer in a shallow dish. Mix dressing with white wine, onion, green pepper, parsley and gherkin and spoon over asparagus. Cover and chill well. To serve, place one-quarter of tomato slices in bottom of a plastic container. Arrange one-quarter of the asparagus spears on top and spoon over one-quarter of the sauce. Seal well and add to the lunch box.
SERVES 4. (70 CALORIES A PORTION.)

HEARTY VEGETABLE SOUP

2 carrots, peeled and sliced
2 sticks celery, chopped
1 onion, chopped
¼ small head cabbage, shredded
500 ml (17 fl oz) water
15 ml (1 tbsp) lemon juice
1 beef stock cube
5 ml (1 tsp) dried mixed herbs
2.5 (½ tsp) dried basil
salt and pepper to taste

Place the vegetables in a large saucepan and add water, lemon juice, stock cube and herbs. Bring to the boil, stirring occasionally, then cover and reduce heat. Simmer for about 1 hour, or until vegetables are tender. Season with salt and pepper if necessary. To pack, heat the required amount, pour into a thermos flask and put in lunch box.
SERVES 5. (62 CALORIES A SERVING.)

CREAM OF VEGETABLE SOUP WITH LEMON

This nutritious soup is equally delicious served hot or cold.

30 g (1 oz) butter
2 onions, thinly sliced
90 g (3 oz) carrots, peeled and sliced
90 g (3 oz) celery, thinly sliced
2 lemons
1 litre (1¾ pints) chicken stock
2 bay leaves
salt and pepper to taste
125 ml (4 fl oz) skimmed milk
chopped fresh parsley to garnish

Melt butter, add vegetables and sauté gently for about 12 minutes, or until soft. Thinly peel the lemons and cut rind into thin strips. Blanch in boiling water for a few minutes, then drain well. Squeeze about 75 ml (5 tbsp) juice from the lemons. Add lemon rind and juice to vegetables. Add stock, bay leaves and season to taste. Bring to the boil, cover and simmer for about 30 minutes, or until vegetables are very soft. Allow the soup to cool for a few minutes, remove bay leaves and purée in a blender or food processor until smooth. Return soup to the pan, stir in milk and reheat. Adjust seasoning.
SERVES 6. (60 CALORIES A PORTION.)

TOMATO YOGHURT SOUP

4 large leeks, finely chopped
4 large tomatoes, peeled and
    chopped
1 bay leaf
5 ml (1 tsp) dried mixed herbs
good pinch dried basil
300 ml (½ pint) water
300 ml (½ pint) low-fat natural
    yoghurt
salt and pepper to taste

Place vegetables in a large saucepan with bay leaf, herbs and water. Cover and simmer over medium heat until vegetables are soft. Remove bay leaf and purée soup in an electric blender or food processor until smooth. Stir in yoghurt and season to taste. Serve hot or cold.
SERVES 4. (57 CALORIES A PORTION.)

BEEF GOULASH ❆

500 g (18 oz) lean stewing steak
20 ml (4 tsp) oil
30 ml (2 tbsp) plain flour
salt and pepper to taste
1 onion, chopped
5 ml (1 tsp) paprika
pinch grated nutmeg
2.5 (½ tsp) dried mixed herbs
1 clove garlic, minced
3 medium tomatoes, peeled and sliced
300 ml (½ pint) beef stock
75 ml (5 tbsp) low-fat natural yoghurt

Cut meat into cubes, removing fat and gristle. Heat oil and brown meat lightly on all sides. Add flour, salt and pepper and stir well. Add chopped onion, paprika, nutmeg, herbs, garlic and tomatoes. Stir in stock and bring to the boil. Turn the mixture into a casserole dish, cover and bake at 180 °C (350 °F, gas 4) for 1¾ hours. At this stage, cool, then refrigerate or freeze goulash. To serve, heat amount needed, stir in some of the yoghurt, spoon into a warmed thermos flask and pack into lunch box.

SERVES 4. (185 CALORIES A PORTION.)

BEEF STROGANOFF ❆

500 g (18 oz) rump steak
20 ml (4 tsp) oil
1 onion, chopped
30 ml (2 tbsp) plain flour
salt and pepper to taste
pinch paprika
10 ml (2 tsp) chopped fresh parsley
300 ml (½ pint) beef stock
60 ml (4 tbsp) tomato purée
150 g (5 oz) mushrooms, sliced
75 ml (5 tbsp) low-fat natural yoghurt

Cut meat into strips, removing any fat. Heat oil in a frying pan, add meat and sauté until well browned. Add onion and sauté for 3–4 minutes, then stir in flour and season with salt, pepper, paprika and parsley. Cook 2 minutes, then stir in stock and tomato purée. Add mushrooms. Bring to the boil, stirring constantly. Turn mixture into a casserole dish and bake at 180 °C (350 °F, gas 4) for about 50 minutes or until meat is tender. If freezing, cool and freeze in individual portions. To serve, heat portions gently, stirring some yoghurt into each. Or, if not freezing, when the stroganoff comes out of the oven, stir in the yoghurt, then cool and refrigerate. Reheat amount needed and pack into warmed thermos flasks.

SERVES 4. (190 CALORIES A PORTION.)

OPEN SALMON SANDWICHES

125 g (4 oz) canned pink salmon, drained and flaked
30 ml (2 tbsp) Slimmers' salad dressing (page 39)
125 g (4 oz) canned water chestnuts, drained and finely chopped
10 ml (2 tsp) chopped onion
2.5 ml (½ tsp) soy sauce
5 ml (1 tsp) lemon juice
3 slices rye bread
3 small tomatoes, sliced

Combine salmon, dressing, water chestnuts, onion, soy sauce and lemon juice. Mix thoroughly and chill. To pack, place 1 slice rye bread in each container. Spread each with one-third of salmon mixture and place tomato on top. Cover container.

SERVES 3. (138 CALORIES A PORTION.)

An Open salmon sandwich, Cucumber and yoghurt salad and an apple make a healthy, slimming lunch

COTTAGE CHEESE SURPRISE SANDWICH

175 ml (6 fl oz) low-fat cottage cheese
1 stick celery, chopped
½ medium carrot, grated
4 radishes, grated
2.5 ml (½ tsp) caraway seeds
10 ml (2 tsp) French or Italian dressing
3 thin slices wholemeal bread
10 ml (2 tsp) butter, softened
3 lettuce leaves
a little paprika

Mash cottage cheese with a fork, then stir in celery, carrot, radishes, caraway seeds and dressing. Chill mixture well. To pack, spread each slice of bread with a little softened butter. Place in a container, topping with a lettuce leaf, then with one-third of the cottage cheese mixture. Sprinkle with a little paprika and cover container. Add to lunch box.

SERVES 3. (138 CALORIES A PORTION.)

BAKED PEARS

4 ripe pears, peeled
150 g (5 oz) canned cranberry sauce
60 ml (4 tbsp) red wine
2.5 ml (½ tsp) ground cinnamon

Cut pears in half lengthwise and remove cores. Place in a saucepan. Mix cranberry sauce, wine and cinnamon and pour over pears. Cover pan and simmer gently until pears are tender, then lift pears out of sauce and cool. When sauce has cooled, spoon it over pears and chill well. To pack, place 2 pear halves in a plastic container and spoon a little sauce over.

SERVES 4. (131 CALORIES A PORTION.)

ORANGE AND BANANA FRUIT SALAD

2 large oranges
4 bananas
30 ml (2 tbsp) lemon juice
15 ml (1 tbsp) orange juice
150 ml (¼ pint) low-fat natural yoghurt
a little sweetener (optional)

Peel oranges and remove pith. Slice into a small bowl. Peel and slice bananas into a small bowl and sprinkle with lemon juice. Fold orange juice into yoghurt and add a little sweetener if desired. Mix oranges, bananas and yoghurt together and chill well before packing in lunch box.

SERVES 4. (117 CALORIES A PORTION.)

MINTY PINEAPPLE

A refreshing dessert to serve for lunch on hot summer days.

675 g (1½ lb) canned pineapple chunks, in natural juice
15 ml (1 tbsp) caster sugar
5 ml (1 tsp) cornflour
4 fresh mint leaves, or 6 drops mint essence
1 drop green food colouring (optional)
6 maraschino cherries, quartered

Drain pineapple, reserving juice. Set the pineapple chunks aside. Combine the pineapple juice, sugar, cornflour and mint leaves. Cook, stirring, until the mixture is bubbling and has thickened. Add green food colouring if desired, then stir in pineapple and cherries. Remove from heat, and chill for several hours before serving. Remove mint leaves before packing in lunch box.

SERVES 5. (82 CALORIES A PORTION.)

NOTE: Minty pineapple will keep well in the refrigerator for 3–4 days.

COCONUT MERINGUES

2 egg whites
pinch salt
few drops vanilla essence
100 g (3½ oz) caster sugar
90 g (3 oz) desiccated coconut

Beat egg whites with salt and vanilla until soft peaks form. Gradually add sugar, beating until stiff peaks form. Fold in coconut. Drop rounded spoonfuls onto a greased baking sheet. Bake at 160 °C (325 °F, gas 3) for about 20 minutes, or until lightly browned. Cool slightly on baking sheet, then remove to a wire rack and cool completely. Store in a tightly covered container.

MAKES 24 MERINGUES. (43 CALORIES EACH.)

CRUNCHY OAT BISCUITS ❄

60 g (2 oz) plain flour
60 g (2 oz) caster sugar
2.5 ml (½ tsp) baking powder
2.5 ml (½ tsp) bicarbonate of soda
2.5 ml (½ tsp) salt
60 g (2 oz) soft brown sugar
60 g (2 oz) butter
1 egg
30 ml (2 tbsp) low-fat natural yoghurt
few drops vanilla essence
90 g (3 oz) rolled oats

Sift flour, white sugar, baking powder, bicarbonate of soda and salt. Beat brown sugar, butter, egg, yoghurt and vanilla essence. Stir into flour mixture and add rolled oats. Mix well, then chill dough for about 1 hour. Drop spoonfuls onto an ungreased baking sheet. Bake at 190 °C (375 °F, gas 5) for about 8 minutes, or until lightly browned. Cool slightly on baking sheet, then remove to a wire rack to cool completely. Store in a tightly covered container. To freeze, pack into freezer containers and seal well.

MAKES 48 BISCUITS. (29 CALORIES A BISCUIT.)

SLIMMERS' LUNCH ADDITIONS

Calculate the total calorie count for your lunchtime menu, then bring it up to about 285 calories by adding one or more of the following healthy snacks:

	CALORIES
1 apple	58
3 fresh apricots	51
¼ melon	39
1 small bunch grapes	40
2 plums	52
1 orange	66
1 peach	42
1 nectarine	31
30 g (1 oz) fresh pineapple chunks	45
250 ml (8 fl oz) skimmed milk	81
125 ml (4 fl oz) low-fat natural yoghurt	57
30 g (1 oz) fresh mushrooms	28
1 large dill pickle	14
5 radishes	4
250 ml (8 fl oz) tomato juice	48
1 small tomato	26
three 5 cm (2 inch) celery sticks	18
three 5 cm (2 inch) carrot sticks	29
60 g (2 oz) raw cauliflower chunks	12
60 g (2 oz) sliced raw courgettes	17
60 g (2 oz) bamboo shoots	27
30 g (1 oz) alfalfa sprouts	38
175 g (6 oz) raw green beans	32
150 g (5 oz) shredded raw cabbage	24
½ medium cucumber	7
1 large green pepper, sliced	22
30 g (1 oz) drained canned asparagus tips	18
1 slice wholemeal bread	30
1 crispbread	31
60 g (2 oz) cooked chicken, no skin	106
60 g (2 oz) drained tuna in brine	102
1 hard-boiled egg	71
125 ml (4 fl oz) low-fat cottage cheese	105

PICNICS AND JOURNEYS

The most important factor to be taken into account when planning the picnic menu, or what food to take on a long car journey, is 'packability'. An elaborate iced cake, for example, may be a family favourite but it will be difficult to pack and, as a result, may look less than beautiful and rather unappetising, by the time you are ready to eat it. All it takes is a little thought and planning, and the right equipment, to ensure the success of any excursion. Our ideas for getting it all together and recipes for great portable foods will leave you with nothing to worry about – except the weather!

PICNICS

Just the suggestion 'let's have a picnic' seems to make life suddenly more carefree. Children are delighted at the prospect of having plenty of space to play in, while grown-ups recall long-past outings with a touch of nostalgia. Food always seems to taste better out-of-doors, possibly because appetites increase in the fresh air. Whether your picnic is impromptu or planned, simple or elaborate, the preparation and presentation should be trouble-free.

PACK IT PERFECTLY

☆ Plan the menu with 'packability' in mind. Foods in their own 'wrappers' – such as oranges, bananas and hard-boiled eggs (kept chilled) – are perfect for picnics as they present no packing problems. Fruit cake, buns, biscuits and cup-cakes pack easily, travel well and look good too.

☆ Pack just enough perishable food for each person, plus a little extra for each person, plus a little for seconds. Fill out the menu with foods that do not spoil easily: breads or crispbreads, fruit and vegetables to nibble and small cakes and biscuits.

☆ Put a little thought into packing the picnic basket. Pack the things you will need last at the bottom and work through the order of use. Place items needed first on top and cover them with the tablecloth. Follow the same order when packing the cool bag.

☆ Cut down on spills by making sure containers are well sealed. It is no joke to open the cool bag and to find the fruit salad all over the sandwiches, so use containers with screw or snap-on tops.

☆ Foil seals more efficiently and insulates much more effectively than clingfilm. Label packets clearly if the shapes are not easily identifiable.

☆ If you are taking breakables, wrap them well. Use towelling face cloths (they can double as napkins) and wrap breakable crockery in the tablecloth.

☆ Don't overlook convenience foods such as prepared dips, salads, cold meats and cheeses. For impromptu picnics, keep a supply of canned fruits, pickles and relishes, prepared pâtés and spreads in your store cupboard.

☆ Remember to leave the picnic area as clean and neat as you would like to find it. If no rubbish bins are provided, collect throw-aways in plastic bags, pack them in the car and dispose of them at home. Pack a large rubbish bag or two. They make cleaning the area easy and can also be used to hold wet swimming gear until you reach home.

CONTAINERS TO CARRY

Good equipment is just as necessary for a successful picnic as planning. Containers play a big part, and there is a wide range to choose from.

Plastics

There is a vast array of plastic containers on supermarket shelves and many are suitable for carrying food on an outing. Choose a variety of sizes and shapes and make sure the lids seal well. These containers are ideal for carrying goodies that don't spoil easily as well as foods like salads, hard-boiled eggs, cold chicken or anything that needs to be placed in a cooler. Small containers are perfect for packing individual meals to stack in the cooler and hand out later.

Baskets

The picnic basket can be as simple as a brightly coloured plastic laundry basket or as elaborate as an elegant wicker hamper fitted with a complete dinner service. Whatever your choice, the basket should be strong, sturdy and large enough to hold all the paraphernalia you want to pack for the picnic. Handles should be well constructed and strong enough not to give way when you carry the full basket.

Coolers

Keeping perishable foods chilled and fresh is a vital part of proper packing for the picnic. An inexpensive polystyrene box can keep chilled food cold for quite some time, provided that the ice or freezing blocks do not melt.

The more expensive insulated metal chest coolers will keep food cold for longer periods. There are even portable electric refrigerators available that operate from the cigarette lighter of the car. And there are insulated bags that work well for cool drinks, fruits and vegetables.

These cool boxes and bags can be used to transport hot foods too. A hot casserole wrapped in foil, then in several layers of newspaper and again in foil will keep hot in an insulated box or chest for about 6 hours. You may wish to have two insulated containers: a large one for cool drinks and chilled food and a smaller one to carry hot casseroles, stews or soups.

The cooling agent in insulated bags or boxes can be as simple as a bag of ice cubes but you will find that a larger, solid block of ice lasts longer and keeps food cooler. To make ice blocks, fill rigid plastic containers two-thirds full of water, leaving room for expansion during freezing. Make sure the lid is on tightly, then freeze. Add the frozen plastic containers to the cooler and you will have no mess as the ice melts. Even easier are the containers of artificial refrigerant available in hardware stores and supermarkets. Freeze the plastic containers and place them in the cooler. They thaw slowly, keeping food chilled for a long time. They are convenient and can be used again.

Thermos containers

Something good to drink is a luxury out-of-doors. Beverages keep at just the right temperature when packed in a thermos flask. You can take a large thermos of cold home-made lemonade, for example, and a smaller one of hot tea or coffee with you.

The increasing availability of thermos containers of various sizes and shapes makes it easy to pack hot or cold beverages, soups and sauces. Wide-mouthed thermos flasks are ideal for packing bulky foods such as hot stews or chilled fruit salad. To help the thermos keep food chilled, fill it with iced water, allow to stand for a while, then drain before adding cold foods. To keep food hot, fill the thermos with boiling water, allow to stand and then drain before adding heated soups or stews.

PICNIC MUSTS

Did you forget the bottle opener on your last picnic? Next time, use this check-list to make sure that indispensable items are packed. If you love going on picnics, it is a time-saving idea to keep a picnic kit handy. Pack it with these essentials:

Openers Can openers, bottle openers and a corkscrew.
Cutlery Knives, forks and spoons (in stainless steel or good re-usable plastic).
Dinnerware Unbreakable plates are best. Try plastic plates or plastic-coated paper plates and add paper plate holders for easier eating.
Glasses Plastic or paper cups. Polystyrene cups work well for hot or cold drinks.
Utensils A small sharp knife, a serrated knife for slicing vegetables and cutting bread and a small cutting board.
Napkins Plenty of paper napkins or a roll of paper towels. Towelling face cloths make colourful and useful napkins – they soak up spills and can be washed.
Condiments Salt, pepper, mustard, tomato ketchup and sugar. Pack them in small unbreakable containers.
Ground or table cover A washable or plastic tablecloth, or a blanket.
Water bottle A bottle of water makes cleaning up easy.
Barbecue If you cook on your outings, keep handy a portable barbecue or grid, long-handled tongs and fork, oven gloves, charcoal, fire starter and matches.
Cleaning up A few large plastic bags take up no space on the way to the picnic and will conveniently hold rubbish on the way home.
First-aid You may wish to add a small first-aid kit to your picnic gear. Include plasters, tweezers, a small bottle of antiseptic for minor cuts and scratches, a bottle of suntan lotion, burn cream and a few pain-killers.

FOR SAFETY'S SAKE

A warm summer's day is perfect for a picnic, but the high temperatures that lure us out can also cause improperly packed foods to spoil. Plan your menu according to the food storage facilities you have. If you have no means of keeping perishable foods cold for 4–6 hours, don't take them! Unless you have a cool bag or an insulated container, avoid taking dairy products, eggs, poultry, fish and shellfish, foods containing mayonnaise (such as potato salad), cream-filled pastries and cream sauces. These foods spoil rapidly unless they are kept chilled.

How you handle foods during and after preparation is important in keeping them fresh. When preparing cold foods, chill them quickly. Do not leave them at room temperature for long periods. Chill or heat foods thoroughly before packing. An insulated or polystyrene container will maintain the temperature of foods for several hours, but cannot heat or chill them. Do not pack hot and cold foods in the same container.

At the picnic site, find a shady place in which to put the insulated container. Keep foods covered except when preparing or serving and keep them out of direct sunlight. Remove chilled or hot foods just before serving and, immediately after eating, return all perishables to the cooler. If there is no ice left, or if there is any possibility that the food may spoil, throw it out. Plan your picnic dishes so that there are few or no leftover perishable foods.

EATING-OUT IDEAS

☆ Use a large green pepper as a container for your favourite dip. Cut off the top, remove the seeds and rinse well. Spoon in the dip, replace top and chill. Wrap in clingfilm and carry to the picnic. Take along crisp, raw vegetables for dipping.
☆ To keep raw vegetables crisp, chill and pack them in a plastic container and add a few ice cubes. The vegetables will keep cool for several hours.
☆ Make individual fruit jellies or instant desserts in plastic or paper cups and chill well. Cover each with clingfilm and pack into an insulated bag. They will stay cold for a number of hours and add a smooth, cool touch to the picnic menu.
☆ Whole fruits are easy to carry, easy to eat and make great desserts. They'll also help dispel the hunger pangs that seem to occur an hour or two after lunch.
☆ Tomatoes make good holders for pasta or potato salad. Cut off top, scoop out pulp (reserve for other use), and fill with salad. Wrap individually, or place in a sealed serving container. Keep cool.
☆ Pack lots of your family's favourite home-made buns or biscuits.
☆ Pack green salad loosely in a plastic bowl with a lid. Pack dressing separately and take along tomato, cumber and onion

---

PICNIC MENUS

Spicy pork chops (page 46)
Spanish salad (page 45)
Crusty bread rolls
Cheesy spread (page 8)
Minty melon bowl (page 48)
Sweet biscuits

Tangy chicken wings (page 46)
Waldorf salad (page 45)
Marinated vegetables (page 46)
Selection of cheeses
Crunchy-topped picnic cake
  (page 48)

Cold roast beef and sauces
  (pages 47–48)
Italian pasta salad (page 45)
Green salad
Delightfully devilled eggs (page 8)
Bread rolls
Marshmallow cup-cakes (page 50)

Parmesan drumsticks (page 46)
Old-fashioned coleslaw (page 46)
Sliced tomatoes
Dill and potato salad (page 46)
Spicy chocolate cake (page 48)

Curried beef rolls (page 47)
Cauliflower salad (page 46)
Vegetable sticks and fromage frais
  dip (pages 8–10)
Chocolate hazelnut brownies
  (page 61)

Bobotie quiche (page 47)
Green salad
Stuffed celery sticks (page 8)
Quick wholemeal loaf (page 18)
Golden peach pie (page 48)

to slice and add just before serving. Add vegetables, pour in dressing, replace lid, invert bowl two or three times, then serve.

☆ An egg carton lined with foil is an ideal carrier for devilled eggs or for small, soft fruits.

☆ Save plastic cottage cheese containers with snap-on lids for packing individual servings of salad or dessert.

WALDORF SALAD

Excellent with cold meats and poultry.

3 red-skinned apples
juice of ½ lemon
5 sticks celery, thinly sliced
225 g (8 oz) seedless green grapes
125 g (4 oz) walnuts, coarsely chopped
125 g (4 oz) Gouda or Edam cheese, grated
45 ml (3 tbsp) seedless raisins
salt and pepper to taste

DRESSING
90 ml (6 tbsp) mayonnaise
30 ml (2 tbsp) clear honey
45 ml (3 tbsp) single cream

Core and slice apples and sprinkle with lemon juice. Place in a large bowl and add celery, grapes, walnuts, cheese and raisins. Season with a little salt and a pinch of pepper. To make dressing, combine all ingredients and mix well. Pour over salad and toss to mix. Transfer to a plastic container with a tightly fitting lid and chill.
SERVES 6.

NOTE: To make this salad a complete meal, add 200 – 300 g (7 – 11 oz) diced cooked chicken or ham, and more mayonnaise to moisten.

SPANISH SALAD

This layered salad marinates on the way to the picnic.

5 firm tomatoes, skinned and sliced
1 cucumber, peeled and sliced
2 green peppers, seeded and diced
1 bunch radishes, sliced
250 g (9 oz) frozen cauliflower, thawed and drained
1 large onion, sliced
20 black olives
salt and pepper to taste

DRESSING
1 clove garlic, crushed
90 ml (6 tbsp) oil
15 ml (1 tbsp) white vinegar
15 ml (1 tbsp) lemon juice
2.5 ml (½ tsp) dried mixed herbs
salt and pepper to taste
15 ml (1 tbsp) chopped fresh parsley
5 ml (1 tsp) chopped chives

In a plastic container with a tightly fitting lid, alternate layers of the prepared vegetables. Season each layer lightly. Add a few olives to some of the layers. To make dressing, combine all ingredients and mix well.
SERVES 8.

ITALIAN PASTA SALAD

200 g (7 oz) small pasta shapes
salt
5 ml (1 tsp) oil
1 green pepper, seeded and chopped
4 tomatoes, peeled and chopped
200 g (7 oz) salami, rind removed, diced

1 small onion, thinly sliced
15 black olives, pitted

DRESSING
125 g (4 oz) blue cheese, crumbled
45 ml (3 tbsp) oil
45 ml (3 tbsp) mayonnaise
20 ml (4 tsp) wine vinegar
pepper to taste
10 ml (2 tsp) chopped fresh parsley
10 ml (2 tsp) chopped fresh basil or 2.5 ml (½ tsp) dried

Cook pasta in boiling salted water for about 12 minutes, or until tender. Drain, rinse with cold water and drain again. Place pasta in a large bowl, add 5 ml (1 tsp) oil and toss to mix. Set aside to cool. When pasta is cool, add green pepper, tomatoes, salami, onion and black olives. Toss lightly to mix. For dressing, blend cheese, 45 ml (3 tbsp) oil, mayonnaise, vinegar, pepper, parsley and basil in a blender. Spoon over pasta, mixing well. Chill for at least 1 hour or until ready to pack the picnic.
SERVES 6.

Waldorf salad (left) and Spanish salad (right) are perfect for picnics

CAULIFLOWER SALAD

1 head cauliflower
3 sticks celery, sliced
300 g (11 oz) frozen green peas, cooked
   and drained
125 g (4 oz) mushrooms, sliced

DRESSING
250 ml (8 fl oz) mayonnaise
1 small onion, finely chopped
60 ml (4 tbsp) soured cream or milk
salt and pepper to taste

Break cauliflower into small florets and place in a large bowl. Add celery, peas and mushrooms. Toss lightly to mix. To make dressing, mix mayonnaise, onion, soured cream or milk, salt and pepper and pour over cauliflower mixture. Toss, then chill for at least 1 hour.
SERVES 8–10.

OLD-FASHIONED COLESLAW

1 small head green cabbage, shredded
1 small onion, finely chopped
125 ml (4 fl oz) chopped canned
   pimiento (red pepper)
125 ml (4 fl oz) soured cream
2 sticks celery, finely chopped
½ small green pepper, seeded and
   chopped
30 ml (2 tbsp) chopped fresh parsley

DRESSING
3 eggs
200 ml (7 fl oz) cider vinegar
15 ml (1 tbsp) dry mustard
10 ml (2 tsp) caster sugar
5 ml (1 tsp) salt
pepper to taste
45 g (1½ oz) butter
30 ml (2 tbsp) plain flour
250 ml (8 fl oz) milk

Combine cabbage, onion, pimiento, soured cream, celery, green pepper and parsley in a large mixing bowl and toss lightly. To make dressing, mix eggs, vinegar, mustard, sugar, salt and pepper and set aside. Melt butter in a heavy saucepan. Stir in flour and cook, stirring, over low heat for about 3 minutes. Do not allow mixture to brown. Gradually stir in milk and cook, stirring, until mixture thickens and just begins to bubble. Reduce heat, and carefully stir in egg mixture. Cook, stirring, until mixture thickens, but do not boil. Remove from heat and cool. Add to salad, tossing to mix well. Cover and refrigerate for up to 3 days.
SERVES 12.

DILL AND POTATO SALAD

1.5 kg (3 lb) potatoes, boiled, peeled and
   cut into bite-sized pieces
1 onion, finely chopped
2 hard-boiled eggs, chopped
1 stick celery, sliced
45 ml (3 tbsp) chopped fresh dill or 20 ml
   (4 tsp) dried
salt and pepper to taste

DRESSING
250 ml (8 fl oz) mayonnaise
10 ml (2 tsp) prepared mustard
10 ml (2 tsp) white vinegar
5 ml (1 tsp) caster sugar

Place the potatoes in a large bowl, add the remaining salad ingredients and toss to mix. To make the dressing, mix mayonnaise with mustard, vinegar and sugar. Pour dressing over the salad and toss lightly again. Transfer to a plastic container with a tightly fitting lid and refrigerate until ready to pack. Keep in the cooler for transporting to the picnic.
SERVES 6–8.

PARMESAN DRUMSTICKS

These are particularly suitable for picnics as they can be eaten with fingers.

2 kg (4½ lb) chicken drumsticks
150 ml (¼ pint) buttermilk
45 ml (3 tbsp) white onion soup powder
45 ml (3 tbsp) plain flour
90 g (3 oz) Parmesan cheese, grated

Dip drumsticks into buttermilk, then into a mixture of the soup powder, flour and parmesan cheese, making sure that they are coated very well. Place drumsticks on a lightly greased baking sheet and chill for about 30 minutes. Bake at 180 °C (350 °F, gas 4) for 45 minutes, then chill again. Carry to picnic in a cooler.
SERVES 8–10.

TANGY CHICKEN WINGS

1 kg (2¼ lb) chicken wings
45 ml (3 tbsp) lime juice
90 ml (6 tbsp) orange juice
60 ml (4 tbsp) oil
30 ml (2 tbsp) grated orange rind
20 ml (4 tsp) finely chopped onion
5 ml (1 tsp) salt
5 ml (1 tsp) dried rosemary
2.5 ml (½ tsp) dried sage
pinch pepper

Place wings in a shallow baking dish. Combine lime and orange juice, oil, orange rind, onion and seasonings and pour over chicken. Bake at 190 °C (375 °F, gas 5) basting several times, for 45–50 minutes or until chicken is tender. Chill wings in sauce, then drain and pack into a container with a tightly fitting lid. Place in cooler.
SERVES 6.

SPICY PORK CHOPS

1 egg
1 clove garlic, crushed
10 ml (2 tsp) prepared mustard
2.5 ml (½ tsp) crumbled dried sage
175 g (6 oz) dried breadcrumbs
salt and pepper
6 pork chops, about 2.5 cm (1 inch)
   thick
60 ml (4 tbsp) oil

Beat egg with garlic and prepared mustard in a shallow dish. Combine sage and breadcrumbs and season with salt and pepper. Dip chops into egg mixture, then into breadcrumb mixture. Chill for 15 minutes, then fry in hot oil in a heavy frying pan over medium-high heat for about 20 minutes, turning once. Chops should be golden brown and no longer pink inside. Drain well, then chill. Pack into a covered container and place in the cooler.
SERVES 6.

MARINATED VEGETABLES

300 g (11 oz) fresh asparagus, broccoli,
   green beans or cauliflower

ITALIAN DRESSING
15 ml (1 tbsp) lemon juice
15 ml (1 tbsp) white vinegar
2.5 ml (½ tsp) dry mustard
pinch dried oregano
1 small clove garlic, finely chopped
15 ml (1 tbsp) chopped fresh parsley
salt and freshly ground black pepper to
   taste
125 ml (4 fl oz) oil

Cook the prepared vegetables in a little boiling water, or steam until just tender. Drain and set aside to cool. To make dressing, combine all ingredients, except oil, and mix well. Beat in oil with a fork or use a blender. Pour the dressing over the cooked vegetables. Chill for a few hours, then drain well and arrange in a serving bowl. Cover tightly, place in a cooler and carry to the picnic.
SERVES 4–6.

CHICKEN LIVER SPREAD ❄

Serve with savoury biscuits or French bread.

60 g (2 oz) butter
½ small onion, chopped
1 clove garlic, crushed
250 g (9 oz) chicken livers
125 g (4 oz) mushrooms, sliced
salt and lemon pepper to taste
1 bay leaf
pinch ground cloves
20 ml (4 tsp) port
60 ml (4 tbsp) natural yoghurt
5 ml (1 tsp) lemon juice

Melt butter in a heavy-based frying pan. Add onion and garlic and sauté until onion is soft. Add chicken livers, mushrooms, salt, lemon pepper, bay leaf and cloves. Cook gently, stirring frequently, until chicken livers lose their pink colour, about 5–8 minutes. Cool slightly, then remove bay leaf. Purée mixture in a food processor with port, half the yoghurt and the lemon juice. Add enough of the remaining yoghurt to make desired consistency. Chill well.
MAKES ABOUT 350 ML (12 FL OZ).

Bobotie quiche and salad

BOBOTIE QUICHE ❄

1 × 23 cm (9 inch) unbaked shortcrust
    pastry shell (see recipe for Golden
    peach pie, page 48)

FILLING
15 ml (1 tbsp) margarine
1 onion, coarsely chopped
10 ml (2 tsp) curry powder
juice of 1 lemon
10 ml (2 tsp) caster sugar
500 g (18 oz) cooked lamb, minced
4 eggs
30 ml (2 tbsp) chutney
30 ml (2 tbsp) ground almonds
30 ml (2 tbsp) raisins
250 ml (8 fl oz) milk
125 ml (4 fl oz) single cream
salt and pepper to taste
a little curry powder

Heat margarine and sauté onion until soft. Add curry powder, lemon juice and sugar. Cook, stirring, for 1 minute. Add to meat with 1 egg, chutney, almonds and raisins. Mix well, then pour into shell. Mix remaining eggs, milk and cream. Season with salt, pepper and extra curry powder. Pour over meat mixture. Bake at 180 °C (350 °F, gas 4) for 35–40 minutes, or until filling has set.
SERVES 6–8.

CURRIED BEEF ROLLS

Make large ones for picnics and smaller ones for journeys and parties.

8 large round bread rolls or 12 smaller
    ones
butter for spreading
20 ml (4 tsp) chopped chives

FILLING
575 g (1¼ lb) corned beef
2.5 ml (½ tsp) curry paste
30 ml (2 tbsp) mayonnaise
10 ml (2 tsp) lemon juice
15 ml (1 tbsp) chutney
salt and pepper to taste
2 small tomatoes, sliced

Cut tops off the rolls and reserve for lids. Remove some of the soft centre, reserve and store for making breadcrumbs. Butter rolls inside and sprinkle with chives. To make filling, mash corned beef and curry paste. Add mayonnaise, lemon juice and chutney and season with salt and pepper. Fill rolls with meat mixture. Place a tomato slice on top of meat mixture in each roll and replace lids. Place in a container or wrap individually and chill.
SERVES 8–12.

COLD ROAST BEEF

Medium-rare roast beef that has been well chilled will be a hit with adults and children alike at a picnic. Arrange beef on a platter, cover and chill. Serve with a choice of sauces and let everyone help themselves. Here are a few suggestions:

CUCUMBER YOGHURT SAUCE
250 ml (8 fl oz) natural yoghurt
90 g (3 oz) cucumber, peeled and seeded
2.5 ml (½ tsp) salt

Place all ingredients in the container of a blender and process until smooth. Chill.
MAKES ABOUT 375 ML (13 FL OZ).

MUSTARD SAUCE
125 ml (4 fl oz) soured cream
15 ml (1 tbsp) prepared mustard
15 ml (1 tbsp) finely chopped onion
salt and pepper to taste

Mix all ingredients well and heat gently in a saucepan for 3 minutes. Chill.
MAKES ABOUT 150 ML (¼ PINT).

HORSERADISH SAUCE

30 ml (2 tbsp) grated horseradish
10 ml (2 tsp) lemon juice
10 ml (2 tsp) caster sugar
pinch dry mustard
125 ml (4 fl oz) single cream

Mix horseradish, lemon juice, sugar and mustard. Whip cream slightly and fold in horseradish mixture. Chill.
MAKES ABOUT 175 ML (6 FL OZ).

MINTY MELON BOWL

1 ripe honeydew melon
2 grapefruit
150 g (5 oz) seedless green grapes

SAUCE
125 ml (4 fl oz) water
100 g (3½ oz) caster sugar
15 ml (1 tbsp) chopped fresh mint
100 ml (3½ fl oz) sweet white wine

Cut melon in half, scoop out seeds and cut flesh into melon balls or bite-sized chunks. Place in a bowl. Peel grapefruit, removing any white pith and divide into segments. Add to melon. Remove stems from grapes and add to melon and grapefruit. To make sauce, heat water and sugar until sugar dissolves, then boil for 5 minutes. Remove from heat, add mint and allow mixture to cool. When sauce is cool, strain to remove mint. Add white wine and pour over fruit. Chill well, stirring occasionally. To carry to picnic, spoon fruit mixture and sauce into a large, wide-mouthed thermos and seal. Tip thermos once or twice to spread sauce evenly before serving.
SERVES 6.

CRUNCHY-TOPPED PICNIC CAKE ✳

300 ml (½ pint) boiling water
90 g (3 oz) rolled oats
125 g (4 oz) margarine, softened
200 g (7 oz) caster sugar
100 g (3½ oz) soft brown sugar
2 eggs
60 ml (4 tbsp) frozen orange juice
    concentrate, thawed
few drops vanilla essence
300 g (11 oz) plain flour
5 ml (1 tsp) baking powder
5 ml (1 tsp) bicarbonate of soda
2.5 ml (½ tsp) salt
2.5 ml (½ tsp) ground cinnamon
good pinch grated nutmeg
pinch ground cloves

TOPPING
100 g (3½ oz) soft brown sugar
60 g (2 oz) margarine
30 ml (2 tbsp) frozen orange juice
    concentrate, thawed
60 g (2 oz) desiccated coconut
60 g (2 oz) pecan nuts, chopped
15 g (½ oz) cornflakes

Pour boiling water over oats in a bowl and set aside. Cream margarine with sugars until light and fluffy. Beat in eggs, one at a time, beating well after each addition. Mix in orange juice concentrate and vanilla. Sift together flour, baking powder, bicarbonate of soda, salt and spices. Stir dry ingredients into creamed mixture alternately with the oat mixture. Spread mixture in a well-greased 23 × 33 cm (9 × 13 inch) baking tin and bake at 180 °C (350 °F, gas 4) for 40–45 minutes, or until a skewer inserted in the centre comes out clean. Cool in the tin on a wire rack. To make topping, combine sugar, margarine and orange concentrate in a saucepan and bring to the boil, stirring. Boil for 1 minute, then remove from heat and stir in remaining ingredients. Spread on cooled cake and place under the grill for 1 minute or until golden brown. At this stage, freeze if desired. Carry the cake to the picnic in the tin and serve cut into squares.
SERVES 16.

SPICY CHOCOLATE CAKE ✳

150 g (5 oz) butter or margarine,
    softened
400 g (14 oz) caster sugar
4 eggs
90 g (3 oz) hot mashed potatoes
60 g (2 oz) plain chocolate, melted
250 g (9 oz) flour
15 ml (1 tbsp) baking powder
5 ml (1 tsp) ground cinnamon
2.5 ml (½ tsp) grated nutmeg
good pinch ground cloves
125 ml (4 fl oz) milk
100 g (3½ oz) hazel nuts, chopped
45 g (1½ oz) seedless raisins (optional)

ICING
90 g (3 oz) plain chocolate
30 g (1 oz) butter or margarine
500 g (18 oz) icing sugar, sifted
about 150 ml (¼ pint) soured cream
pinch salt
few drops vanilla essence

Beat butter or margarine and sugar together until fluffy. Add eggs one at a time, beating well after each addition. Add potatoes and chocolate and mix well. Sift flour with baking powder and spices and add to creamed mixture alternately with milk. Beat until smooth, then stir in nuts and raisins. Spread mixture in a greased and floured 23 × 33 cm (9 × 13 inch) baking tin and bake at 180 °C (350 °F, gas 4) for 35–40 minutes, or until skewer inserted in the centre comes out clean. Cool in the tin on a wire rack. To make icing, melt chocolate and butter together. Remove from heat and cool to room temperature. In a large mixing bowl, mix icing sugar with half the soured cream, the salt and vanilla. Stir in chocolate mixture and add enough of the remaining soured cream to make a spreading consistency. Use to ice cooled cake. Freeze if desired. Serve cut into squares.
SERVES 16.

GOLDEN PEACH PIE

SHORTCRUST PASTRY
175 g (6 oz) plain flour
pinch salt
5 ml (1 tsp) caster sugar
125 g (4 oz) butter
1 egg yolk
about 45 ml (3 tbsp) cold water

FILLING
750 g (1¾ lb) canned sliced peaches,
    drained
100 g (3½ oz) caster sugar
30 ml (2 tbsp) plain flour
good pinch grated nutmeg
pinch ground cinnamon
pinch salt
30 g (1 oz) butter
15 ml (1 tbsp) lemon juice
2.5 ml (½ tsp) grated orange rind
few drops almond essence

To make pastry, sift flour with salt and sugar. Rub in butter until mixture resembles fine crumbs. Combine egg yolk and water and add enough to dry ingredients to form a soft dough. Roll out half the pastry and use to line a 23 cm (9 inch) pie dish. Roll out remaining pastry for the crust. To make filling, drain peaches, reserving 125 ml (4 fl oz) syrup. Combine sugar, flour, nutmeg, cinnamon and salt. Add reserved syrup and cook, stirring, until mixture thickens. Add butter, lemon juice, orange rind, almond essence and peaches. Spoon into pie dish. Moisten edges of pastry shell and place pastry for crust on top. Trim, seal and flute edge. Cut four slashes in crust. Bake at 200 °C (400 °F, gas 6) for 40–50 minutes. If pastry browns too quickly, fold foil loosely around edge. Cool pie on a wire rack. Serve at room temperature.
SERVES 6–8.

Round off the picnic with Spicy chocolate cake

JOURNEYS

It is always a good idea to take some tasty and convenient food for the road when you're setting off on a long journey. Taking food with you instead of buying it along the way saves time and money but does require some careful advance planning. Choose items that will be the easiest and least messy to eat on the move. Finger foods are fast and save packing cutlery and plates – in any case, it's not easy to balance a dinner plate on your lap when you eat.

When planning meals to eat on the road, remember that an insulated bag does double duty by keeping food chilled and beverages cold. The same pointers apply for keeping perishable foods fresh on the road as for the picnic, so read 'For Safety's Sake' in the picnic section of this chapter.

Pack meals in individual containers to hand out as you drive along. Use brown paper bags or individual plastic containers that will fit comfortably in the insulated bag. Wrap, then pack sandwiches, cold chicken, vegetables, fruits, biscuits or cup-cakes. It's an easy way to serve a meal and avoids squabbles among the children over the biggest sandwich or biscuit. Purchase individual cartons of fruit juice, take some straws with you, and you will have a ready solution to the 'I want a drink' problem.

Some easy-to-pack and non-messy snacks to take along for the ride are grapes, bananas, cucumber pieces, oranges ready peeled and segmented, cubes of cheese, popcorn, granola, dry chunky cereals, biscuits, cakes and bars. Take fabric place-mats along to cover laps while you eat – they are large enough to do the job really well and they're washable. Take plenty of napkins or paper towels. Pre-moistened wipes are just right for cleaning messy fingers or giving a refreshing wipe to a hot, sticky face. And don't forget the plastic bag for collecting empty wrappings and beverage containers to dispose of later.

See 'School Break' (pages 7–10), 'The Great Sandwich' (pages 11–16) and 'Pack and Send' (pages 60–62) for ideas.

THE SWEET TOOTH

Tucked into thousands of lunch boxes and bags that go off to school and work every morning is something sweet to look forward to – a biscuit, a piece of cake or a home-made sweet. These remedies for sweet-tooth cravings will provide a delightful finish to a packed meal, quick energy for the long afternoon and also some nutrients, as many of them are full of fruits, nuts and cereals.

Drop biscuits and bars can withstand a reasonable amount of rough treatment, as can individual tarts, fairy cakes and cup-cakes. They are therefore ideal additions to make to the lunch box, so make one of these your choice for something to sweeten the day.

This chapter provides recipes for sweet treats that travel well. Many of them survive well in the freezer, so make up a couple of batches and wrap individually before freezing.

ALMOND ORANGE POUNDCAKE ❄

Bake these cakes in two loaf tins, then slice and wrap individual slices for storing in the freezer. When you need a sweet treat for lunch, take one directly from the freezer and place it in the lunch box.

500 g (18 oz) plain flour
5 ml (1 tsp) salt
10 ml (2 tsp) baking powder
500 g (18 oz) butter
575 g (1¼ lb) granulated sugar
8 eggs
250 ml (8 fl oz) milk
few drops vanilla essence
few drops almond essence
30 ml (2 tbsp) orange juice

Sift flour with salt and baking powder and set aside. Cream butter and gradually add sugar, beating until mixture is light and fluffy. Add eggs, one at a time, beating well after each addition. Mix milk, vanilla, almond essence and orange juice and add to creamed mixture alternately with flour, starting and ending with flour. Line two 10 × 20 cm (4 × 8 inch) loaf tins with greased parchment and divide mixture between them. Bake at 180 °C (350 °F, gas 4) for about 1 hour or until a skewer inserted in the centre comes out clean. Allow cakes to cool in tins for 15–20 minutes, then lift them out and cool them on wire racks. To freeze for the lunch box, slice cakes, wrap each slice in clingfilm and freeze on a tray. When frozen, slices can be placed in a rigid container.
MAKES 2 LOAVES.

CARROT BISCUITS ❄

350 g (12 oz) plain flour
15 ml (1 tbsp) baking powder
225 g (8 oz) margarine, melted
100 g (3½ oz) soft brown sugar
100 g (3½ oz) granulated sugar
2 eggs
150 ml (¼ pint) puréed cooked carrots
few drops vanilla essence
few drops lemon essence
5 ml (1 tsp) grated orange rind

GLAZE
60 ml (4 tbsp) orange juice
20 ml (4 tsp) grated orange rind
300 g (11 oz) icing sugar

Sift flour and baking powder together into a mixing bowl and set aside. In a large bowl, add melted margarine to brown sugar, white sugar, eggs, carrots, vanilla, lemon essence and grated orange rind. Beat until smooth. Gradually stir in flour mixture to form a smooth, soft dough. Chill dough for at least 1 hour. The dough can be refrigerated for up to 3 days before baking. Drop rounded spoonfuls of mixture 5 cm (2 inches) apart on a greased baking sheet. Bake at 190 °C (375 °F, gas 5) for 10–12 minutes. Allow to cool for 1 minute on baking sheet, then remove to wire rack set over waxed paper. To make glaze, combine orange juice and rind in a bowl. Stir in enough icing sugar to form a thick, smooth mixture. While biscuits are still warm, coat each with glaze. To freeze, first open-freeze, then pack into containers, seal well and freeze.
MAKES 96 BISCUITS.

MARSHMALLOW CUP-CAKES ❄

The marshmallows rise during baking to form a crusty icing. These cup-cakes will be a favourite with the younger generation – and with sweet-toothed adults!

175 g (6 oz) chocolate, melted
250 g (9 oz) plain flour
7.5 ml (1½ tsp) bicarbonate of soda
2.5 ml (½ tsp) salt
125 g (4 oz) butter, softened
300 g (11 oz) soft brown sugar
3 eggs
few drops vanilla essence
125 ml (4 fl oz) water
60 g (2 oz) miniature marshmallows (or large marshmallows, chopped)

Allow chocolate to cool to room temperature. Sift flour with bicarbonate of soda and salt and set aside. With an electric mixer, beat butter until creamy. Gradually add sugar, mixing until well blended. Add eggs, one at a time, beating well after each addition. Stir in vanilla. At low speed, stir in flour mixture, water and melted chocolate. Beat until dry ingredients are just moistened, then increase speed and beat at medium speed for 3 minutes. Stir in marshmallows by hand. Fill paper cups in bun tins two-thirds full and bake at 180 °C (350 °F, gas 4) for 20 minutes, or until a skewer inserted in the centre comes out clean. Cool cup-cakes on a wire rack. To freeze, wrap individually, freeze, then pack into a rigid container, seal well and place in freezer.
MAKES 30 CAKES.

GINGERBREAD ✳

Cut into small squares, gingerbread tastes good with coffee or a glass of milk.

125 g (4 oz) butter, melted
100 g (3½ oz) granulated sugar
1 egg, beaten
300 g (11 oz) plain flour
7.5 ml (1½ tsp) bicarbonate of soda
5 ml (1 tsp) ground cinnamon
5 ml (1 tsp) ground ginger
2.5 ml (½ tsp) salt
10 ml (2 tsp) grated orange rind
150 g (5 oz) molasses
150 g (5 oz) clear honey
250 ml (8 fl oz) hot water
25 ml (5 tsp) orange juice

Allow butter to cool to room temperature, then add sugar and egg and beat well. Sift flour with bicarbonate of soda, cinnamon, ginger and salt. Combine orange rind, molasses, honey, hot water and orange juice. Add flour mixture to butter mixture alternately with molasses mixture. Mix well, then place in a well-greased 23 cm (9 inch) square baking tin and bake at 180 °C (350 °F, gas 4) for 1 hour. Cool in tin, on a wire rack. When cool, cut into small squares and wrap each in clingfilm. Freeze on a tray, then place in a freezer container. Pack a frozen square in the lunch box.
MAKES 20 SMALL SQUARES.

CANDIED ORANGE PEEL

3 medium oranges
1 litre (1¾ pints) cold water
15 ml (1 tbsp) salt
400 g (14 oz) granulated sugar
125 ml (4 fl oz) water
extra sugar

Cut oranges into quarters, remove the flesh and save it for another purpose. Remove pith from rind. Place cold water in a large bowl, add salt and rind. Weigh down with a plate to keep rind under water and allow to stand overnight. Drain rind and wash thoroughly in cold water. Cover rind with cold water and heat to boiling. Drain. Repeat procedure three times, to remove bitter taste. Cut rind into thin strips. Combine 300 g (11 oz) rind with sugar and 125 ml (4 fl oz) water. Cook, stirring, until sugar dissolves. Continue cooking until rind is translucent. Drain thoroughly and roll in sugar. Dry on a wire rack and store in a covered container. To pack, wrap a few pieces in clingfilm and add to lunch box.
MAKES ABOUT 450 G (1 LB).

CHEESECAKE BARS

All the flavour of cheesecake in an easy-to-pack bar.

75 g (2½ oz) butter or margarine
75 g (2½ oz) soft brown sugar
125 g (4 oz) plain flour
60 g (2 oz) hazelnuts, finely chopped

FILLING
60 ml (4 tbsp) caster sugar
250 g (9 oz) cream cheese
1 egg
few drops vanilla essence
30 ml (2 tbsp) milk
15 ml (1 tbsp) lemon juice
10 ml (2 tsp) finely grated lemon rind

Cream butter and brown sugar until fluffy. Stir in flour until mixture resembles fine crumbs. Add nuts, mixing well. Reserve 250 ml (8 fl oz) mixture and press remainder into a greased 20 cm (8 inch) square baking tin. Bake at 180 °C (350 °F, gas 4) for 12 minutes. To make filling, beat sugar and cheese until fluffy. Add egg, vanilla, milk, lemon juice and rind. Beat until smooth. Spoon cheese mixture evenly over cooked base and sprinkle with remaining crumb mixture. Return to the oven and bake for 25 minutes, or until filling has set. Allow to cool, then cover and refrigerate. To pack, cut into squares, wrap in clingfilm and place in lunch box.
MAKES 16 BARS.

CHERRY DROPS

90 g (3 oz) packet vanilla pudding mix
  (not instant)
200 g (7 oz) granulated sugar
150 ml (¼ pint) evaporated milk
15 g (½ oz) butter or margarine
few drops vanilla essence
few drops caramel essence
60 g (2 oz) nuts, chopped
45 ml (3 tbsp) chopped glacé cherries
12 glacé cherries, halved

In a saucepan, combine pudding mix, sugar and evaporated milk. Cook, stirring, until the mixture boils, then boil for 5 minutes, stirring constantly. Remove from heat, add butter, vanilla and caramel. Beat with an electric mixer at high speed for 3–4 minutes, or until mixture holds its shape. Stir in nuts and chopped cherries. Drop spoonfuls of mixture onto a greased baking sheet and top each with a cherry half. Allow to set. Store in a cool place.
MAKES 24 CHERRY DROPS.

HONEY BISCUITS ✳

125 g (4 oz) butter, softened
100 g (3½ oz) granulated sugar
150 g (5 oz) clear honey
1 egg
30 ml (2 tbsp) milk
175 g (6 oz) plain flour
5 ml (1 tsp) salt
2.5 ml (½ tsp) ground cinnamon
pinch ground allspice
pinch grated nutmeg
2.5 ml (½ tsp) bicarbonate soda
30 g (1 oz) shredded wheat cereal,
  crumbled
60 g (2 oz) nuts, chopped
100 g (3½ oz) raisins

Beat together the butter, sugar, honey, egg and milk until well mixed. Sift the flour with salt, cinnamon, allspice, nutmeg and bicarbonate of soda. Add dry ingredients to butter mixture, stirring until well blended. Stir in cereal, nuts and raisins. Drop spoonfuls of mixture onto greased baking sheets and bake at 190 °C (375 °F, gas 5) for 12–14 minutes or until lightly browned. Cool slightly on the baking sheet, then remove to a wire rack and cool completely. Store tightly covered, or freeze.
MAKES 60 BISCUITS.

DATE AND RAISIN ROUNDS ✳

125 g (4 oz) butter
100 g (3½ oz) granulated sugar
60 g (2 oz) brown sugar
1 egg
few drops vanilla essence
125 g (4 oz) plain flour
2.5 ml (½ tsp) baking powder
good pinch bicarbonate of soda
good pinch grated nutmeg
2.5 ml (½ tsp) salt
75 g (2½ oz) raisins
100 g (3½ oz) pitted dates, chopped
90 g (3 oz) sugared cereal flakes,
  crushed

Combine butter, brown and white sugar, egg and vanilla and beat well. Sift flour with baking powder, bicarbonate of soda, nutmeg and salt. Gradually add to butter mixture, mixing well. Stir in raisins and dates. Drop spoonfuls of date mixture into crushed cereal, rolling to coat well. Place about 5 cm (2 inches) apart on an ungreased baking sheet and bake at 190 °C (375 °F, gas 5) for 10–12 minutes. Cool on a wire rack and store in a tightly covered container, or freeze.
MAKES ABOUT 36 ROUNDS.

CINNAMON SUGAR CAKES ✳

250 g (9 oz) plain flour
5 ml (1 tsp) baking powder
5 ml (1 tsp) bicarbonate of soda
pinch salt
125 g (4 oz) butter, softened
200 g (7 oz) granulated sugar
2 eggs
few drops vanilla essence
250 (8 fl oz) soured cream

TOPPING
100 g (3½ oz) caster sugar
60 ml (4 tbsp) plain flour
pinch ground cinnamon
30 g (1 oz) butter or margarine

Sift flour, baking powder, bicarbonate of soda and salt together and set aside. With an electric mixer, beat butter until creamy, then gradually add sugar, beating well. Add eggs, one at a time, beating well after each addition. Add the vanilla and beat until light and fluffy. On low speed, stir in flour mixture alternately with soured cream, beginning and ending with flour. Fill paper bun cups in tins two-thirds full with batter. To make topping, combine sugar, flour and cinnamon and rub in butter. Sprinkle over batter. Bake at 180 °C (350 °F, gas 4) for 20–25 minutes, or until a skewer inserted in the centre comes out clean. Remove cupcakes from tins and cool on a wire rack. To freeze, wrap individually, freeze, pack into a rigid container, seal and replace in freezer.
MAKES 30 CAKES.

ALMOND TARTS ✳

300 g shortcrust pastry (see recipe for Golden peach pie, page 48)

FILLING
1 egg white
pinch salt
75 g (2½ oz) icing sugar
45 g (1½ oz) ground almonds
few drops almond or vanilla essence
75 ml (5 tbsp) raspberry or strawberry jam
sliced almonds

Clockwise from front: Chocolate peanut bars, Almond tarts and Cinnamon sugar cakes

Roll out pastry and line fluted tart tins. Chill pastry while making the filling. To make filling, beat egg white with salt until soft peaks form. Gradually beat in icing sugar, a little at a time, beating after each addition. Beat until well blended and thick. Stir in ground almonds and almond or vanilla essence. Spoon 2.5 ml (½ tsp) jam into each tart, then spoon 5 ml (1 tsp) filling over jam. Top each tart with a sliced almond. Bake at 190 °C (375 °F, gas 5) for about 25 minutes, or until topping is puffy and golden. Carefully remove tarts from tins and allow to cool on a wire rack. When cool, store in a tightly sealed container or wrap individually and freeze on a baking sheet, then pack into freezer containers.
MAKES 26 TARTS.

MERINGUE-TOPPED FAIRY CAKES

350 g (12 oz) plain flour
15 ml (1 tbsp) baking powder
2.5 ml (½ tsp) salt
150 g (5 oz) butter, softened
300 g (11 oz) granulated sugar
3 eggs
few drops vanilla essence
300 ml (½ pint) milk

TOPPING
2 egg whites
pinch salt
100 g (3½ oz) soft brown sugar
45 g (1½ oz) nuts, finely chopped

Sift flour, baking powder and salt together and set aside. Beat butter at medium speed with an electric mixer until creamy. Gradually add granulated sugar and beat until well blended. Add eggs, one at a time, beating well after each addition. Add the vanilla and beat until mixture is light and fluffy. At low speed, stir in flour mixture alternately with milk, beginning and ending with flour. Line bun tins with paper cups and fill each about two-thirds full with batter. Bake at 180 °C (350 °F, gas 4) for 20 minutes. To make the topping, beat egg whites with salt until frothy. Gradually beat in sugar until mixture is stiff.

When cakes are done, remove from the oven, spread a little meringue mixture on each and sprinkle with nuts. Increase temperature to 220 °C (425 °F, gas 7) and return cakes to oven to bake for a further 3–5 minutes, or until tops are lightly browned. Remove from tins and cool on wire rack. To freeze, wrap individually, open-freeze, then pack into rigid containers.
MAKES 30 CAKES.

SURPRISE MUFFINS ✳

These muffins are made with just two ingredients – ice-cream and flour. Vary the flavour by using different ice-cream.

250 g (9 oz) self-raising flour
500 ml (17 fl oz) soft vanilla ice-cream

Combine flour and ice-cream in a mixing bowl and beat until smooth. Fill greased bun tins three-quarters full and bake at 220 °C (425 °F, gas 7) for 20–25 minutes or until golden brown. These muffins freeze well. Wrap each in clingfilm and freeze until firm. Place in freezer container.
MAKES 12 MUFFINS.

CHOCOLATE NUT CRUNCHIES

Bite-sized treats to satisfy any sweet tooth.

175 g (6 oz) plain chocolate
10 ml (2 tsp) butter
60 ml (4 tbsp) smooth peanut butter
30 ml (2 tbsp) icing sugar
125 g (4 oz) bite-size shredded wheat cereal
45 g (1½ oz) peanuts, finely chopped

Place chocolate and butter in top of a double boiler and melt over hot water. Stir in peanut butter and sugar. Carefully dip shredded wheat pieces into chocolate and place on a wire rack. Sprinkle with nuts and allow to cool. Store in an airtight container in a cool place.
MAKES 125 G (4 OZ).

CHOCOLATE PEANUT BARS

90 g (3 oz) butter
100 g (3½ oz) soft brown sugar
60 ml (4 tbsp) golden syrup
few drops vanilla essence
175 g (6 oz) rolled oats
90 g (3 oz) plain chocolate
75 ml (5 tbsp) peanut butter
45 g (1½ oz) peanuts, chopped

Cream butter and sugar until well mixed. Add golden syrup, vanilla and oats. Spread in a greased 23 cm (9 inch) square baking pan and bake at 180 °C (350 °F, gas 4) for about 15 minutes, or until well set. Remove from oven and allow to cool. Melt together chocolate and peanut butter and spread over the base. Sprinkle with peanuts. Chill before cutting into bars.
MAKES 16 BARS.

FILL THE FREEZER

If you've gone through the Monday morning drama of hunting in the fridge for bits of Sunday's roast to make sandwiches for lunch and then discovered that someone forgot to buy bread, you need to read this chapter. You will find out how to become organised, plan ahead and get going. Have a sandwich session, cook up casseroles, batch-bake biscuits and cakes and store them in the freezer.

Many recipes in this book display the freezer symbol ❄ which indicates that they are suitable for freezing. In this chapter you will find guide-lines for packing, freezing and serving. Containers, ideal storage times and thawing are also discussed.

FREEZER TIPS

☆ Seasonings taste stronger after freezing, so be sparing with salt, pepper, garlic and spices.

☆ Divide foods for the freezer into quantities that you will use at one time, then wrap. Label each package with contents and any special instructions, such as addition of seasoning, reheating, number of servings and so on.

☆ Label containers with the date to keep track of how long foods have been in the freezer. Use foods in rotation, so that nothing stays in the freezer longer than the recommended time.

☆ Be sure food is well wrapped and correctly packaged before freezing. The cold air in the freezer will dry out any foods that are not covered, causing deterioration of quality and flavour.

☆ Fast-freeze foods by placing them in the coldest part of the freezer, but make sure air can circulate around them. After items are frozen, stack them for convenient storing.

☆ Open-freeze small items or individual servings – sandwiches, slices of pâté or cake – by placing on a tray in the freezer until solid. They can then be wrapped before freezing for later use.

☆ When packing foods that are high in liquid content – soups, stews, soft dips or spreads – leave 2.5 cm (1 inch) head space in the container to allow for expansion during freezing.

PACKAGING

Selecting containers and packaging materials for freezing is very important as they affect the quality of the frozen food.

Freezer containers and packaging materials should be easy to handle and stack, take up little freezer space and protect the food while it is in the freezer. Packaging materials should prevent the loss of moisture from food and keep air out. They should be durable and not split or leak at low temperatures.

Here is a rundown on the most popular types of freezer packaging materials:

FOIL

Heavy-duty foil is best for freezer use as it is more resistant to splitting and tearing than ordinary foil. Foil can easily be moulded to fit the shape of the food and if the edges are folded over securely, the package will be airtight. Foil can, however, be punctured or torn in the freezer, so it may be best to overwrap using freezer paper, or a plastic bag.

FOIL CONTAINERS

Some of these containers are just the right size for individual servings of stew or for small quiches and tarts. There is a wide variety of sizes and shapes on the market and some have waxed paperboard lids to seal in freshness. If no lid is provided, seal well with heavy-duty foil and overwrap if desired.

PLASTIC FREEZER CARTONS

These are easy to use and to keep clean. They come in a wide variety of sizes and shapes and most have snap-on or screw-on lids that make them airtight. The initial purchase of a selection of good plastic freezer containers may be costly but, if they are properly cared for, they will last for years.

Sandwich-sized containers can go directly from freezer to lunch box and save packing and repacking sandwiches.

PLASTIC BAGS

Use thick, heavy bags for large quantities or items and thinner ones for sandwiches, biscuits and snack foods. Plastic bags are available in various sizes. To pack food for the freezer, mould the bag to the shape of the food, pressing out as much air as possible, then fasten securely. Sandwiches and snack foods can go directly from freezer to lunch box in their own plastic bags and will thaw and be ready to eat by lunch time.

COOKING BAGS

These are very useful for storing small quantities of casseroles, soups and stews that need to be reheated before packing for lunch. All that has to be done is to place the sealed, frozen bag in a saucepan of boiling water, heat food through, then open the bag and tip the hot food into a warmed, wide-mouthed thermos flask and seal. You'll have a quick and easy hot lunch in no time at all and with no mess.

WAXED CARTONS

Cardboard cartons with a waxed interior are ideal if you have a microwave oven. Select the size and shape needed, fill with individual portions of stew or casserole, close with the lid and freeze. To reheat, place directly in the microwave from the freezer, heat, then tip into wide-mouthed thermos flasks that have been warmed in advance with boiling water and seal to keep hot until lunch time.

CLINGFILM

It is best to use special freezer clingfilm because ordinary clingfilm may not stay sealed if used in the freezer. If you do use ordinary clingfilm, overwrap or tape it to keep air out.

INTERLEAVING SHEETS

It is worth investing in a roll of these specially treated thin plastic sheets if you bulk-freeze, as they keep foods from sticking together when frozen. Using them makes it easy to pack individual portions of cake, pâté, sandwiches and so on in a bulk bag and it is simple to remove what you need and reseal the packet. Interleaving sheets are re-usable. You can also use a double layer of waxed paper to keep frozen foods from sticking together, but the waxed paper cannot be used again and is not as effective as the interleaving sheets.

FREEZER LABELS

It is important to label food parcels that are to be frozen so that you know what they are. Use special freezer labels if possible, as ordinary labels may fall off the packets in the freezer. Alternatively, you can write directly on the bags or containers with wax pencil or an indelible felt-tip marker.

FREEZER GUIDE-LINES

BREADS

Both home-made and commercially baked breads freeze well. As with any food that goes into the freezer, it is important that the bread is fresh when you freeze it, as freezing can prolong, but not improve, freshness. Remember that slicing bread before freezing will save on thawing time and frozen sliced bread can be buttered straight from the freezer when making sandwiches.

How to freeze

Wrap loaves and sliced bread well in freezer or plastic bags, seal, label and freeze.

Cool freshly baked rolls, muffins or scones, then place in plastic bags or freezer containers, seal, label and freeze. To use, take out what you need and reseal the container.

How to thaw

Remove bread from the freezer and leave it in its wrappings at room temperature until thawed. Thawing time varies according to the size and shape of the loaf and can be as long as 3 hours. Sliced bread, rolls, muffins and scones can be placed on a plate and covered with clingfilm to thaw. They take up to 20 minutes to thaw at room temperature.

Storage time

As a general rule, unsliced and sliced bread, muffins, scones and rolls can be stored in the freezer for 2–3 months.

French bread, as well as other loaves and rolls with a crisp crust, should remain in the freezer no longer than 2–3 weeks.

CAKES

Plain cakes and cakes with butter icing freeze very well. It is best not to freeze cakes with royal or glacé icing because this becomes sticky when it thaws. Cream or fruit fillings may make the cake soggy when thawed, so don't freeze them either.

Always use fresh, good quality ingredients when making cakes for storing in the freezer. Remember that flavourings may change during freezing, so use a little less spice, vanilla or almond essence. For best results, cool cakes completely before packaging and freezing.

How to freeze

Small cakes such as cup-cakes and fairy cakes may be open-frozen, individually wrapped, then packed into freezer containers, sealed and labelled. To use, remove as many as you need and re-seal the container. Whole, plain cakes must be cooled completely before freezing. They can be stacked in twos interleaved with plastic or waxed paper. Place in plastic bags or freezer containers, extract air, seal and label.

Open freeze iced cakes, then wrap them in foil or place them in a freezer bag, seal and label. To keep iced cakes from getting damaged in the freezer, it is a good idea to place the frozen, wrapped cake in a rigid container.

Slices of iced cake can be frozen individually. Here again, you are able to take out only as many as you need. Open-freeze the slices, then wrap in foil or place in sandwich bags. Place slices in a freezer container, seal and label.

How to thaw

Thaw cakes at room temperature. Small cakes take 30–60 minutes, large cakes can take up to 2½ hours to thaw. To thaw iced cakes, remove wrappings, place on a plate and cover with a cake tin, plastic container or dome to keep moisture from condensing on the icing. Thaw large or small un-iced cakes in their wrappings at room temperature.

Storage time

Most cakes will keep for as long as 3–4 months in the freezer but, if they are iced, they should be used within 2 months. Cup-cakes and fairy cakes keep well for about 2 months but spice cakes should be used within 6 weeks.

BISCUITS, BARS AND COOKIES

How to freeze

Bake biscuits as usual and cool completely. Pack into freezer containers with waxed paper between layers and on top of the last layer. Seal, label and freeze. It's a good idea, if a little time-consuming, to wrap biscuits and cookies in twos back to back and to wrap bars individually before packing in freezer containers.

How to thaw

If biscuits, bars or cookies are to be packed in the lunch box, take them directly from the freezer, wrap (if they are not individually wrapped) and place in the lunch box. Otherwise, thaw biscuits, bars and cookies in their wrappings at room temperature for 30 minutes.

Storage time

Biscuits, bars and cookies will keep well in the freezer for 2–3 months.

PASTRY DISHES

SAVOURY AND SWEET PIES, QUICHES AND PIZZAS

Baked pastry dishes are never quite as crisp and tasty after freezing as they are when freshly cooked but individual portions of meat pies, pasties, pizzas, quiches or sweet tarts do make satisfying additions to the packed lunch.

How to freeze

Make pies and tarts, flans and quiches, pasties and pizzas according to recipe directions. Use individual foil flan dishes where possible to make serving easy.

Brush the inside of pastry for savoury dishes with melted butter and the inside of pastry for sweet dishes with a little beaten egg white before baking. This will help keep the pastry crisp. Bake dishes as the recipes direct, then cool quickly. Flans, quiches and pizzas may be cut into serving portions and individually wrapped before freezing. They can be added to the lunch box frozen and will be just right for eating by lunch time. Wrap the cooked, cooled foods well, seal, label and freeze.

You can also freeze individual pizzas uncooked, then quickly bake them in the morning before packing lunch. They won't stay hot, but they will have a fresher taste. Make the bases, add toppings, wrap well in foil and freeze. Pizzas can go directly into the oven from the freezer; just peel the top foil back.

How to thaw
Leave items in their wrappings at room temperature. Individual portions take about 45 minutes to thaw; whole pies, quiches and so on, may take 2½–3 hours. Individual servings may be packed directly in the lunch box and will thaw by lunch time. If any of these cooked dishes are to be reheated before eating, unwrap, place on a baking sheet and heat through in the oven at 180 °C (350 °F, gas 4).

Storage time
Pastry dishes with sweet or savoury fillings store well in the freezer for up to 3 months.

MAIN-COURSE DISHES

SOUPS, STEWS AND CASSEROLES
Soups, stews and casseroles can be pre-cooked and frozen for later use. Be sure to pack them in amounts you will use at one time and in packaging materials that will be most convenient for you. Individual portions frozen in dishes suitable for microwave cooking make reheating easy. Packing portions into cooking bags allows you to reheat with the least effort and mess.

Don't put mixtures with high vinegar, wine or tomato content in aluminium containers, as these substances may discolour the containers and the flavour may be affected. Pasta should not be frozen in casseroles, soups or stews – it will go soggy when thawed and reheated. Make up and freeze the base or sauce, then add the pasta when reheating the mixture. Potatoes cooked in stews and casseroles can go very mushy and watery during freezing, so it would be safer to use recipes that don't contain them when cooking for the freezer.

Cream or soured cream in main-course dishes may curdle or separate during freezing, so stir these in when reheating.

How to freeze
Prepare stews and soups according to recipe but, if they must be reheated before serving, slightly undercook any vegetables they may contain. Spoon mixtures into containers, seal, label and freeze.

How to thaw
If you wish to thaw dishes before reheating, it is best to let them thaw in the refrigerator for several hours or overnight.

Many stews, casseroles and soups can be reheated from frozen in a microwave oven or in the top of a double boiler over simmering water. Stir as little as possible during reheating. Tip into wide-mouthed, insulated bottles and seal to keep hot for lunch.

Storage time
Casseroles, stews and soups can be stored for up to 2 months in the freezer.

SAVOURIES

DIPS, SPREADS, PATES AND TERRINES
Dips and spreads that have fromage frais or cream as a base freeze well, although they may need to be stirred when thawed. Make according to recipe directions but leave out ingredients that contain a lot of water, such as celery, cucumber or tomato. Stir these into the mixture when thawed. Pâtés, loaves and terrines made with meat, liver or fish freeze well. Pack and freeze in small containers or in individually wrapped slices to pack for lunch.

How to freeze
Pack dips and spreads in conveniently sized containers, leaving a little headspace to allow for expansion during freezing. Seal, label and freeze.

Cool pâtés quickly and pack into small freezer container. Terrines and meat loaves, once cool, may be sliced and reassembled, with interleaving sheets placed between the slices. Wrap well, seal and label, then freeze.

How to thaw
Dips and spreads are best thawed overnight in the refrigerator but small amounts can be thawed in the lunch box, then stirred before using. Pâtés, meat loaves and terrines can be thawed in the refrigerator overnight or at room temperature for about 2 hours.

Storage time
All of the above have a freezer storage time of 1 month.

SANDWICHES
Bread, buns and rolls usually freeze very well, as do many sandwich fillings, so there is no excuse for serving the same lunchtime selection over and over again. Have a sandwich session and make it easy on yourself – prepare, wrap and freeze enough sandwiches for 2–3 weeks and pack the sandwiches of your choice each morning.

Sandwich fillings that freeze well include those made with cream cheese, cottage cheese, hard cheeses, hard-boiled egg yolk, sliced or minced cooked meat and poultry, tuna, salmon, sardines, fish paste, peanut butter, nuts, dried fruits, olives and pickles.

It is best not to freeze sandwich fillings containing a lot of mayonnaise as it may separate when thawed. However, small amounts of mayonnaise can be used to bind filling ingredients and shouldn't cause any problems. Soured cream, pineapple or orange juice, apple sauce and cream cheese make good binders for sandwich fillings that are to be frozen. Other items that should not be used as fillings for sandwiches that are to be frozen include hard-boiled egg white (it may discolour and become leathery) and salad ingredients that contain a lot of water, such as lettuce, tomato, celery and cucumber.

How to freeze
Make sandwiches in the usual way. Cut, then individually wrap sandwiches in sandwich bags, freezer clingfilm or foil. Pack into freezer containers. Seal, label and freeze. Open-freeze open sandwiches on a tray, then wrap well and place in suitable freezer containers.

How to thaw
Sandwiches should be thawed, wrapped, at room temperature. Take them from the freezer and pack directly in the lunch container. They will have thawed by lunch time and will taste just as good as when they were made.

Storage time
Store open sandwiches for no longer than 1 month, closed sandwiches for 6 weeks to 2 months – they will lose their freshness if you store them for longer.

AVOCADO AND YOGHURT SOUP ❄

2 large ripe avocados
juice of 1 lemon
400 ml (14 fl oz) chicken stock
125 ml (4 fl oz) natural yoghurt
dash Tabasco
salt and lemon pepper to taste
10 ml (2 tsp) chopped chives
125 ml (4 fl oz) milk

Peel avocados and cut in half. Remove stones and mash flesh with lemon juice. Place in a blender or food processor, add stock, yoghurt, Tabasco, seasoning and chives. Blend until smooth. To freeze, pour into freezer containers, seal well, label and freeze. To thaw, leave in refrigerator overnight. To pack for lunch, stir a little milk into each serving, pour into a thermos flask and seal. Serve chilled.
SERVES 4.

CREAMY CARROT SOUP ❄

A pinch of allspice and grated orange rind add an unusual flavour.

500 g (18 oz) carrots, peeled and sliced
1 small onion, chopped
750 ml (1¼ pints) chicken stock
salt and pepper to taste
10 ml (2 tsp) caster sugar
1 bay leaf
1 stick celery, finely chopped
2.5 ml (½ tsp) dried mixed herbs
pinch ground allspice
thinly peeled rind of ½ orange
juice of ½ orange
150 ml (¼ pint) single cream

Place all the ingredients, except the cream, in a large saucepan and simmer for about 30 minutes, or until vegetables are tender. Remove bay leaf and orange rind and cool until lukewarm. Purée carrot mixture in a blender or food processor and allow to cool completely. To freeze, package soup in individual portions if desired, seal well, label and freeze. To thaw, place in a saucepan and heat gently, then pour into a wide-mouthed thermos flask and stir in 30 ml (2 tbsp) cream for each serving.
SERVES 4–5.

CHEESE AND ONION QUICHE ❄

150 g (5 oz) shortcrust pastry (see recipe for Golden peach pie, page 48)
10 ml (2 tsp) melted butter

FILLING
1 large onion, finely chopped
200 g (7 oz) Cheddar cheese, grated
2.5 ml (½ tsp) dried mixed herbs
salt and black pepper to taste
good pinch dry mustard
3 eggs
175 ml (6 fl oz) milk
60 ml (4 tbsp) single cream

Roll out pastry and line a 23 cm (9 inch) pie dish. Brush pastry with melted butter. To make filling, mix all ingredients and spoon into pastry shell. Bake at 190 °C (375 °F, gas 5) for 35–40 minutes, or until a knife inserted in the centre comes out clean. Place pie dish on wire rack to cool. To freeze, cut into serving wedges and wrap each in foil, sealing well. Overwrap, if desired, label and freeze. To thaw, allow portions to stand, wrapped, at room temperature for about 1 hour.
SERVES 6–8.

Curried pork with apricots

COUNTRY PORK TERRINE

15 g (½ oz) butter
15 ml (1 tbsp) plain flour
150 ml (¼ pint) milk
pinch grated nutmeg
pinch ground cloves
125 g (4 oz) pork belly, rind removed
125 g (4 oz) pork liver
1 small onion
1 clove garlic
100 g (3½ oz) sausagemeat
salt and black pepper to taste
1 bay leaf

Melt butter in a saucepan, stir in flour and cook, stirring, for 1 minute. Gradually stir in milk. Cook, stirring, until thickened and bubbly. Season with nutmeg and cloves and set aside. Finely mince pork belly, liver, onion and garlic and mix well. Combine with sausagemeat, salt and pepper. Add reserved sauce and mix well. Turn mixture into a greased and lined loaf tin and place bay leaf on top. Cover with foil and place in a roasting tin. Add water to come half-way up the sides of the loaf pan and bake at 180 °C (350 °F, gas 4) for 1 hour. Cool in the tin before turning out. Chill overnight. To freeze, slice and separate slices with greaseproof paper. Wrap well in foil and overwrap in a plastic bag if desired. Seal, label and freeze. To thaw, remove as many slices as desired and wrap in foil. The slices will thaw but still be cool by lunch time. Pack crusty French bread or several savoury biscuits with the terrine.
MAKES 1 TERRINE THAT SLICES INTO 8–10 PORTIONS.

CURRIED PORK WITH APRICOTS ❄

1 kg (2¼ lb) lean pork, cubed
30 ml (2 tbsp)
1 onion, chopped
10 ml (2 tsp) curry powder, or to taste
30 ml (2 tbsp) plain flour
400 ml (14 fl oz) beef stock
125 g (4 oz) dried apricots, quartered
45 g(1½ oz) sultanas
½ green pepper, sliced
salt and pepper to taste
30 ml (2 tsp) chutney

Heat the oil, brown meat on all sides, then remove meat from pan. Add onion to oil and sauté until it is just tender. Stir in curry powder and flour and cook, stirring, for 1 minute. Gradually stir in stock, bring to the boil, then reduce heat. Simmer for about 5 minutes, stirring occasionally. Return meat to pan, add apricots, sultanas and green pepper and season with salt and pepper. Cover and simmer over low heat until meat is tender, about 1 hour. About 15 minutes before end of cooking time, stir in chutney. To freeze, chill curry, then place in a large freezer container or pack into individual containers or cooking bags and seal, label and freeze. To thaw, allow to stand at room temperature overnight, then reheat. Individual portions that have been frozen in cooking bags may be reheated in simmering water, then tipped into wide-mouthed thermos flasks and sealed to keep hot until lunch time.
SERVES 6.

SALMON PASTIES ※

30 g (1 oz) butter
30 ml (2 tbsp) chopped onion
30 g (1 oz) plain flour
150 ml (¼ pint) milk
225 g (8 oz) canned salmon, drained and
   flaked
salt and pepper to taste
20 ml (4 tsp) lemon juice
10 ml (2 tsp) chopped fresh parsley
750 g (1¾ lb) frozen puff pastry,
   thawed
beaten egg

Melt butter in a frying pan and sauté onion until just tender. Add flour and cook, stirring, for 1 minute. Gradually stir in the milk. Bring to the boil and cook, stirring, for 2 minutes. Add salmon, salt and pepper, lemon juice and parsley. Mix well and cool. Roll out pastry and cut eight oval or circular shapes, then cut eight slightly smaller shapes. Divide salmon mixture between the eight smaller shapes. Dampen edges of all the pastry shapes, then cover the smaller ones with the larger ones. Seal edges. To freeze, first open-freeze, then pack into freezer containers, seal, label and freeze. To use, place frozen pasties on a lightly greased baking sheet, brush with beaten egg and bake at 200 °C (400 °F, gas 6) for 20 minutes. Reduce heat to 180 °C (350 °F, gas 4) and bake 20 minutes more. Serve hot or cold.
MAKES 16 SMALL PASTIES.

SMOKED MACKEREL PATE ※

350 g (12 oz) smoked mackerel
125 ml (4 fl oz) fromage frais
200 g (7 oz) butter, melted
20 ml (4 tsp) prepared horseradish
juice of 1 large lemon
10 ml (2 tsp) chopped fresh dill
45 ml (3 tbsp) single cream
pepper to taste

Discard skin and bones from fish and mash flesh. Stir in fromage frais and half the melted butter. Add remaining ingredients, mixing well. To freeze, spoon into a serving dish, foil dish or individual serving dishes and smooth top. Spoon on remaining melted butter and chill until butter has set. Wrap and seal well, label and freeze. To thaw, leave at room temperature for about 4 hours. Individual servings will thaw in about 2½ hours. Serve with French bread, home-made wholemeal bread or savoury biscuits.
SERVES 4–6.

CHEESY SCONES ※

125 g (4 oz) plain flour
7.5 ml (1½ tsp) baking powder
2.5 (½ tsp) salt
pinch white pepper
2.5 ml (½ tsp) dry mustard
45 g (1½ oz) butter or margarine
60 g (2 oz) Cheddar cheese, grated
15 ml (1 tbsp) chopped fresh parsley
2.5 ml (½ tsp) dried mixed herbs
1 small egg, beaten
a little milk

Sift flour, baking powder, salt, pepper and mustard into a mixing bowl. Rub in butter until mixture resembles breadcrumbs. Add cheese, parsley and herbs. Add egg and enough milk to make a soft dough. Turn out onto a floured surface and knead lightly, then roll or pat into a circle about 2.5 cm (1 inch) thick. Place dough on a greased baking sheet and brush with a little milk. Mark into six wedges with a knife.

Bake at 200 °C (400 °F, gas 6) for 12–15 minutes, or until golden brown. Cool on a wire rack, then cut into wedges. To freeze, wrap the wedges individually, seal well, label and freeze. Wedges will thaw in about 30 minutes at room temperature.
SERVES 6.

VARIATION
You can create an interesting flavour variation – and make these scones almost a meal in themselves – by adding 10 ml (2 tsp) finely minced onion and 90 g (3 oz) ham, finely chopped, to the dry ingredients before mixing in the beaten egg and milk.

MOCHA TRUFFLES ※

125 g (4 oz) plain chocolate
15 ml (1 tbsp) milk
15 ml (1 tbsp) golden syrup
125 g (4 oz) butter, softened
125 g (4 oz) icing sugar, sifted
10 ml (2 tsp) instant coffee powder
60 g (2 oz) cocoa powder
pinch mixed spice

Place chocolate, milk and syrup in a small saucepan and heat gently until chocolate has melted. Remove from heat and set aside to cool. Beat in butter, icing sugar, coffee powder, half the cocoa and the mixed spice. Beat until light and fluffy, then slowly beat in melted chocolate mixture and continue beating until mixture is very fluffy and pale in colour. Chill for at least 1 hour, then form into balls. Roll balls in remaining cocoa powder. To freeze, place in a freezer container, seal, label and freeze. To thaw, leave covered in the refrigerator overnight or at room temperature for about 2 hours.
MAKES ABOUT 24 TRUFFLES.

CHERRY AND ALMOND LOAF CAKE ※

225 g (8 oz) glacé cherries
225 g (8 oz) plain flour
15 ml (1 tbsp) baking powder
2.5 ml (½ tsp) salt
175 g (6 oz) margarine, softened
175 g (6 oz) caster sugar
3 eggs
few drops vanilla essence
90 g (3 oz) flaked almonds

Rinse cherries and pat dry, then cut in half and toss in a little of the flour. Sift together flour, baking powder and salt. Combine margarine, sugar, flour mixture, eggs and vanilla in a large mixing bowl and mix well. Fold in cherries and half the flaked almonds. Spoon mixture into a well-greased and floured 1 kg (2¼ lb) loaf tin and sprinkle with remaining almonds, pressing in lightly. Bake at 160 °C (325 °F, gas 3) for 1 hour 45 minutes, or until a skewer inserted in the centre comes out clean. Turn out onto a wire rack to cool. To freeze, slice if desired, then reassemble, with greaseproof paper placed between slices. Wrap well, seal, label and freeze. To thaw, allow whole loaf to stand in wrappings at room temperature for about 3 hours. Individual slices may be wrapped, frozen and placed in the lunch box. They will thaw by lunch time.
MAKES ONE 1 KG (2¼ LB) LOAF THAT CUTS INTO 12–14 SLICES.

HONEY CHEESECAKE ※

Rich dessert for lunch, or to take on a picnic.

CRUST
225 g (8 oz) digestive biscuits, crushed
90 g (3 oz) butter, melted
2.5 ml (½ tsp) ground cinnamon

FILLING
500 ml (17 fl oz) fromage frais
45 ml (3 tbsp) clear honey
60 ml (4 tbsp) soft brown sugar
pinch salt
juice of 1 lemon
3 eggs, beaten
ground cinnamon

To make crust, combine crushed biscuits, melted butter and cinnamon, mixing well. Press mixture into the base and sides of a 20 cm (8 inch) spring-form tin and chill. To make filling, cream the fromage frais, honey, sugar and salt in a large bowl. Beat in lemon juice, then beat in eggs, one at a time, mixing well after each addition. Beat until mixture is light and fluffy. Spoon filling into prepared crumb base and bake at 160 °C (325 °F, gas 3) for 35–45 minutes, or until filling has set. Turn off oven and allow cheesecake to cool completely in oven. When cool, sprinkle with cinnamon. To freeze, remove from tin, open-freeze, then wrap in foil and overwrap in a plastic bag. To freeze individual portions, cut cooled cheesecake into wedges, open-freeze, wrap well and pack into freezer container. To thaw the whole cake, unwrap, place on a serving dish and leave in the refrigerator for 5 hours or overnight. To thaw portions, loosen wrap and leave at room temperature for about 1 hour.

SERVES 6–8.

INDIVIDUAL MINCE PIES ❄

A rich dessert to complement a light starter or main course.

PASTRY
175 g (6 oz) butter
125 g (4 oz) caster sugar
2 egg yolks
10 ml (2 tsp) brandy
pinch salt
275 g (10 oz) plain flour

FILLING
500 g (18 oz) mincemeat
grated rind of 1 lemon
1 apple, peeled, cored and grated
10 ml (2 tsp) lemon juice
30 ml (2 tbsp) brandy
icing sugar

To make pastry, add butter, sugar, egg yolks, brandy and salt to flour and mix to a soft dough using a mixer. Chill in the refrigerator for 1 hour. To make filling, combine mincemeat, lemon rinds, apple, lemon juice and 30 ml (2 tbsp) brandy in a mixing bowl. Roll pastry out thinly and cut 18 fluted circles. Use the circles

Honey cheesecake

to line 18 greased tartlet tins. Divide filling between pastry shells. Cut 18 slightly smaller circles and place on top of mincemeat. Flute edges and pierce the top of each pie twice with a skewer. Bake at 180 °C (350 °F, gas 4) for 20–25 minutes, or until golden. Allow pies to cool on a wire rack. To freeze, allow pies to cool completely, then pack in layers in a freezer container with layers of waxed or greaseproof paper between layers of pies. Seal, label and freeze. To thaw, remove from freezer, sprinkle with icing sugar, wrap well and leave at room temperature for about 45 minutes.

MAKES 18 MINCE PIES.

DATE NUT BREAD ❄

Delicious spread with butter at tea time or as an in-between snack. Spread with a fromage frais filling (see 'The Great Fromage Frais Dip', pages 8–10) to make a delicate, unusual sandwich.

45 ml (3 tbsp) golden syrup
30 g (1 oz) butter or margarine
60 ml (4 tbsp) caster sugar
150 g (5 oz) plain flour
7.5 ml (½ oz) baking powder
2.5 ml (½ tsp) salt
good pinch ground cinnamon
pinch grated nutmeg
pinch ground cloves
125 g (4 oz) dates, pitted and chopped
60 g (2 oz) nuts (such as walnuts or hazel nuts), chopped
1 egg, beaten
30 ml (2 tbsp) milk

Place syrup, butter or margarine and caster sugar in a small saucepan and heat over low heat until butter has melted. Remove from heat. Sift flour, baking powder, salt cinnamon, nutmeg and cloves into a large mixing bowl. Stir in chopped dates and nuts, the syrup mixture, beaten egg and milk. Mix well, then spoon the mixture into a well-greased 23 × 13 cm (9 × 5 inch) loaf tin. Bake at 160 °C (325 °F, gas 3) for 40–45 minutes, or until a skewer inserted in the centre of the loaf comes out clean. Turn out onto a wire rack to cool. To freeze, cool completely, then slice if desired and reassemble, placing waxed or greaseproof paper between slices. Wrap well, label and freeze. Thaw in wrappings at room temperature for about 3 hours. Frozen slices will thaw much more quickly than a whole loaf and may be spread with butter while still frozen, wrapped, added to the lunch box, and be ready for eating by tea time.

MAKES 1 LOAF THAT CUTS INTO 12–14 SLICES.

PACK AND SEND

Home-baked goodies make thoughtful personal gifts to send to friends and loved ones far away. Children at boarding school, students and those in the armed forces will really appreciate a little taste of home while they are away.

Bear in mind that the baked goods could be subjected to rough treatment and be damaged during transportation and take this into account when selecting what to bake and send. Treats that travel well under most conditions are bars, biscuits and sweets. Soft biscuits generally travel better than crisp ones, so choose those that you know will stand up to the journey. Avoid sending thin, fragile biscuits – they may crumble before reaching their destination and cause great disappointment. Icing does not travel well, so top bars and squares with icing sugar instead.

The recipes in this chapter are all for bars and biscuits that can be sent on their way without fear of crumbling. As long as you are careful when wrapping and packing them, they should arrive at their destination fresh and good enough to eat.

Other good travellers, for which recipes can be found elsewhere in this book are: Molasses squares, page 35; Raisin nuggets, page 36; Carrot biscuits, page 50; Date and raisin rounds, page 51; Honey biscuits, page 51 and Cinnamon sugar cakes, page 53.

PACKING MATERIALS

You will need a sturdy container. A heavy cardboard box or a rigid plastic or metal container such as a biscuit tin will do the job. Line the container with waxed paper or foil and have plenty of filler to hand. Crushed or shredded waxed paper, clingfilm, tissue paper or newspaper will prevent the biscuits from being crushed; puffed cereal and popped popcorn can also be used to cushion the biscuits.

WRAPPING THE BISCUITS

Wrap biscuits in pairs, back to back, with a little piece of waxed paper between them. Wrap bars individually. Use a moisture-proof material such as plastic or clingfilm to hold in the flavour while the goodies make their journey.

PACKING THE BISCUITS

Pad the bottom of the container with crushed paper, then pack biscuits snugly in rows. Place the heaviest ones at the bottom if you are sending more than one kind. Cover each layer with a cushion of padding material. Place an especially fat layer of padding material on the top. The box should be so full that you have to press down gently to get the lid on. And, of course, don't forget to include a card to say who sent them.

WRAP AND LABEL

Tape the lid shut and print the name and address of the recipient on the container. Wrap the container tightly in heavy-duty brown paper and tie securely with cord. Print the name and address of recipient and sender plainly on the package and label the parcel 'Fragile', 'Perishable', and 'Handle with care'.

NOUGAT SQUARES ❄

30 g (1 oz) butter
2 eggs, lightly beaten
200 g (7 oz) soft brown sugar
75 ml (5 tbsp) flour
2.5 ml (½ tsp) baking powder
few drops vanilla essence
45 g (1½ oz) walnuts, chopped

Place butter in a 20 cm (8 inch) square baking tin and melt in the oven at 180 °C (350 °F, gas 4). Mix remaining ingredients and spread in the tin. Bake at 180 °C (350 °F, gas 4) for about 25 minutes, until lightly browned and set. Cool in tin on wire rack for 5 minutes, then cut into squares. Allow to cool completely, then sprinkle with icing sugar if desired. Store tightly covered, or freeze.
MAKES 16 SQUARES.

FRUIT MINCE SQUARES ❄

These are easy to make and freeze well.

300 g (11 oz) soft brown sugar
2 eggs
30 ml (2 tbsp) molasses
15 g (½ oz) butter
few drops vanilla essence
250 g (9 oz) plain flour
2.5 ml (½ tsp) salt
2.5 ml (½ tsp) bicarbonate of soda
5 ml (1 tsp) ground cinnamon
2.5 ml (½ tsp) ground cloves
45 ml (3 tbsp) hot water
45 g (1½ oz) flaked almonds
60 g (2 oz) sultanas
175 g (6 oz) mincemeat
icing sugar

Beat sugar, eggs, molasses, butter and vanilla well. Sift flour with salt, bicarbonate of soda and spices and stir into sugar mixture, sultanas and mincemeat. Spread dough in two 23 × 33 cm (9 × 13 inch) baking tins and bake at 200 °C (400 °F, gas 6) for 12–15 minutes. Allow to cool slightly. Cut into squares and cool completely. Sprinkle with icing sugar and store in a tightly covered container or freeze.
MAKES 72 SQUARES.

ORANGE SPICE SQUARES ❊

Moist, delicious and easy to bake.

150 g (5 oz) butter
200 g (7 oz) soft sugar
1 egg
15 ml (1 tbsp) grated orange rind
60 ml (4 tbsp) orange juice
300 g (11 oz) plain flour
5 ml (1 tsp) bicarbonate of soda
2.5 ml (½ tsp) salt
2.5 ml (½ tsp) grated nutmeg
2.5 ml (½ tsp) ground cinnamon
150 g (5 oz) sultanas
100 g (3½ oz) mixed chopped peel
60 ml (4 tbsp) chopped glacé
   cherries
60 ml (4 tbsp) chopped, pitted dates

Beat butter, sugar and egg until fluffy. Mix in orange rind and juice. Sift flour with bicarbonate of soda, salt, nutmeg, cinnamon and stir into mixture. Mix in sultanas, peel, cherries and dates and spread evenly in two greased 23 cm square baking tins. Bake at 200 °C (400 °F, gas 6) for 15–18 minutes. Test to see if cake is done; if it is, the top will spring back when lightly touched. Cool slightly in tins, then cut into squares and cool completely. If desired, sprinkle with icing sugar. Store in a tightly covered container or freeze.
MAKES 32 SQUARES.

CHOCOLATE HAZELNUT BROWNIES ❊

125 g (4 oz) butter
60 g (2 oz) plain chocolate
2 eggs
200 g (7 oz) caster sugar
90 g (3 oz) plain flour
pinch salt
2.5 ml (½ tsp) baking powder
few drops vanilla essence
45 g (1½ oz) hazelnuts, chopped

Melt butter and chocolate over hot water. Stir to mix. Beat eggs well, then add sugar gradually, beating constantly. Add slightly cooled chocolate mixture, mixing well. Stir in vanilla and nuts. Spread mixture in a greased 23 × 33 cm (9 × 13 inch) baking tin and bake at 160 °C (325 °F, gas 3) for 20 minutes, until a skewer inserted in the middle comes out clean. Cool in tin, then cut into squares. Sprinkle with icing sugar if desired. Store in a tightly covered container or freeze.
MAKES 24 BROWNIES.

BLONDE BROWNIES ❊

90 g (3 oz) butter
200 g (7 oz) soft brown sugar
2 eggs
175 g (6 oz) plain flour
5 ml (1 tsp) baking powder
pinch salt
90 g (3 oz) plain chocolate, grated
45 g (1½ oz) pecan nuts, chopped

Beat butter, brown sugar and eggs together well. Sift flour with baking powder and salt and add to butter mixture, mixing well. Stir in chocolate and nuts and spread mixture in a greased, 23 cm (9 inch) square baking tin. Bake at 180 °C (350 °F, gas 4) for 30 minutes. Cool in the tin and when almost cool, cut into bars. Store in a tightly covered container or freeze.
MAKES 16 BROWNIES.

PEANUT BUTTER BISCUITS ❊

125 g (4 oz) peanut butter
60 g (2 oz) butter or margarine
100 g (3½ oz) soft brown sugar
100 g (3½ oz) caster sugar
1 egg, beaten well
125 g (4 oz) plain flour
5 ml (1 tsp) bicarbonate of soda

Cream peanut butter with butter. Add the sugars gradually, beating until mixture is light and fluffy. Add beaten egg and mix well. Sift flour with bicarbonate of soda and add to peanut butter mixture, mixing in well. Drop spoonfuls of the mixture onto a lightly greased baking sheet. Press each down with floured prongs of a fork. Bake at 180 °C (350 °F, gas 4) for 10–12 minutes. Cool on a wire rack. When cool, store in a tightly covered container or freeze.
MAKES 48 BISCUITS.

SPICY NUT BISCUITS ❊

125 g (4 oz) butter
250 g (9 oz) soft brown sugar
1 egg
few drops vanilla essence
300 g (11 oz) plain flour
10 ml (2 tsp) baking powder
2.5 ml (½ tsp) salt
good pinch ground ginger
2.5 ml (½ tsp) ground cinnamon
good pinch ground cloves
2.5 (½ tsp) grated nutmeg
45 g (1½ oz) pecan nuts, chopped
48 pecan halves for decoration

Combine butter, sugar, egg and vanilla and beat until light and fluffy. Sift flour with baking powder, salt and spices and mix into creamed mixture. Stir in chopped pecan nuts. Chill mixture for 15–20 minutes, then roll the dough into balls. Place about 5 cm (2 inches) apart on greased baking sheets. Place a pecan half on top of each biscuit, pressing down slightly. Bake at 190 °C (375 °F, gas 5) for 10–12 minutes. Cool on a wire rack, then store in a tightly covered container or freeze.
MAKES 48 BISCUITS.

OAT AND BANANA BISCUITS ❊

175 g (6 oz) butter
200 g (7 oz) caster sugar
1 egg, beaten
175 g (6 oz) plain flour
2.5 ml (½ tsp) bicarbonate of soda
5 ml (1 tsp) salt
5 ml (1 tsp) ground cinnamon
good pinch grated nutmeg
150 g (5 oz) rolled oats
2–3 ripe bananas, mashed
75 g (2½ oz) raisins

Beat all ingredients in a mixing bowl until well blended. Drop spoonfuls 2.5 cm (1 inch) apart onto an ungreased baking sheet. Bake at 200 °C (400 °F, gas 6) for about 12 minutes. Cool on a wire rack. Store in a tightly covered container or freeze.
MAKES 48 BISCUITS.

CHEWY WALNUT BARS ❊

90 g (3 oz) butter, melted
150 g (5 oz) caster sugar
45 g (1½ oz) soft brown sugar
1 egg
few drops vanilla essence
60 g (2 oz) plain flour
5 ml (1 tsp) baking powder
2.5 ml (½ tsp) salt
2.5 ml (½ tsp) ground cinnamon
125 g (4 oz) walnuts, chopped

Add butter to sugars and beat well. Add egg and vanilla and mix well. Sift together flour, baking powder, salt and cinnamon and add to creamed mixture. Stir in nuts and spread batter in a well-greased 20 cm (8 inch) square baking tin. Bake at 180 °C (350 °F, gas 4) for 20 minutes. Cool in the tin for 5 minutes, then cut into bars. Cool completely, remove bars and store in a tightly covered container or freeze.
MAKES 16 BARS.

TOFFEE BARS ✳

BASE
125 g (4 oz) butter, softened
100 g (3½ oz) soft brown sugar
125 g (4 oz) plain flour

TOPPING
2 eggs
200 g (7 oz) soft brown sugar
few drops vanilla essence
30 ml (2 tbsp) plain flour
5 ml (1 tsp) baking powder
2.5 ml (½ tsp) salt
90 g (3 oz) desiccated coconut
15 ml (1 tbsp) water
45 g (1½ oz) flaked almonds

To make base, mix the butter with the sugar and flour and press into an ungreased 23 × 33 cm (9 × 13 inch) baking tin. Bake at 180 °C (350 °F, gas 4) for 10 minutes. To make topping, beat eggs and stir in sugar and vanilla. Mix in flour, baking powder and salt. Moisten coconut with 15 ml (1 tbsp) water and add to egg mixture. Add almonds, and mix in. Spread over base, return to oven for 25 minutes or until topping is golden. Cool slightly, then cut into bars. Cool completely, then store in a tightly covered container or freeze.

MAKES 24 BARS.

ORANGE COCONUT FINGERS ✳

125 g (4 oz) butter
200 g (7 oz) soft brown sugar
1 egg
few drops vanilla essence
few drops lemon essence
30 ml (2 tbsp) milk
125 g (4 oz) plain flour
2.5 ml (½ tsp) salt
10 ml (2 tsp) baking powder
2.5 ml (½ tsp) ground cinnamon
90 ml (6 tbsp) desiccated coconut
30 ml (2 tbsp) finely chopped candied orange peel

Combine butter, sugar, egg, vanilla, lemon essence and milk, beating well. Sift flour with salt, baking powder and cinnamon. Stir into butter mixture. Stir in coconut and candied peel and spread mixture in a lightly greased, 23 cm (9 inch) square baking tin. Bake at 160 °C (325 °F, gas 3) for 30–35 minutes or until golden brown. Cool in tin for 2–3 minutes; cut into fingers. Cool completely, then store in a tightly covered container or freeze.

MAKES 40 FINGERS

FRUIT CAKE BISCUITS ✳

100 g (3½ oz) soft brown sugar
60 g (2 oz) butter
2 eggs
175 g (6 oz) plain flour
2.5 ml (½ tsp) ground cinnamon
2.5 ml (½ tsp) ground allspice
2.5 ml (½ tsp) grated nutmeg
2.5 ml (½ tsp) bicarbonate of soda
45 ml (3 tbsp) milk
350 g (12 oz) pecan nuts, chopped
250 g (9 oz) mixed dried fruit
75 g (2½ oz) sultanas
100 g (3½ oz) glacé cherries, chopped
60 ml (4 tbsp) whisky, sherry or brandy

Beat sugar and butter until fluffy. Add eggs and beat well. Sift flour with cinnamon, allspice and nutmeg and add to sugar mixture. Mix bicarbonate of soda with milk and add to sugar mixture with fruit and nuts. Mix well, then stir in whisky, sherry or brandy. Drop spoonfuls onto a lightly greased baking sheet and bake at 180 °C (350 °F, gas 4) for 10–15 minutes. Do not bake too long: biscuits should still be soft. Cool on baking sheet for 2 minutes, then remove to a wire rack and cool completely. Store in a tightly covered container, or freeze.

MAKES 48 BISCUITS.

SUGARED LEMON BALLS ✳

225 g (8 oz) butter or margarine
200 g (7 oz) soft brown sugar
1 egg
15 ml (1 tbsp) grated lemon rind
10 ml (2 tsp) lemon juice
175 g (6 oz) plain flour
2.5 ml (½ tsp) bicarbonate of soda
2.5 ml (½ tsp) cream of tartar
pinch salt
good pinch ground ginger
caster sugar

In a large mixing bowl, beat butter with sugar and egg until fluffy. Stir in lemon rind and juice. Sift flour, together with bicarbonate of soda, cream of tartar, salt and ginger and stir into butter mixture. Chill mixture in the refrigerator for about 15 minutes, then roll into balls, 2.5 cm (1 inch) in diameter. Roll each ball in sugar, then place balls on an ungreased baking sheet. Bake at 180 °C (350 °F, gas 4) for about 10 minutes, or until lightly browned. Cool on a wire rack, then store in a tightly covered container or freeze.

MAKES 36 BALLS.

RAISIN DROP BISCUITS ✳

300 g (11 oz) seedless raisins
250 ml (8 fl oz) water
475 g (17 oz) plain flour
5 ml (1 tsp) baking powder
5 ml (1 tsp) bicarbonate of soda
5 ml (1 tsp) salt
2.5 ml (½ tsp) ground cinnamon
2.5 ml (½ tsp) grated nutmeg
225 g (8 oz) butter
375 g (13 oz) caster sugar
3 eggs, lightly beaten
few drops vanilla essence
45 g (1½ oz) pecan nuts or walnuts, coarsely chopped

Bring raisins and water to boil in a saucepan. Boil for 3 minutes, then cool. Sift flour, baking powder, bicarbonate of soda, salt and spices together in a mixing bowl and set aside. Beat butter and sugar until light and fluffy, then add eggs and vanilla and mix well. Stir in raisins and any remaining water. Gradually add flour mixture, beating well after each addition. Stir in nuts. Drop spoonfuls 2.5 cm (1 inch) apart onto an ungreased baking sheet. Bake at 190 °C (325 °F, gas 5) for 12–15 minutes. Cool on a wire rack, then store in a tightly covered container or freeze.

MAKES 36 LARGE OR 72 SMALL BISCUITS

SOURED CREAM BISCUITS

These biscuits are rich and good, and enough to feed a crowd.

100 g (3½ oz) caster sugar
100 g (3 ½ oz) soft brown sugar
125 g (4 oz) butter
125 ml (4 fl oz) soured cream
1 egg
few drops vanilla essence
200 g (7 oz) plain flour
2.5 ml (½ tsp) ground cinnamon
2.5 ml (½ tsp) bicarbonate of soda
2.5 ml (½ tsp) salt
45 g (1½ oz) bran flakes
90 g (3 oz) sultanas

Cream sugars and butter until light and fluffy, then beat in soured cream, egg and vanilla. Stir together the flour, cinnamon, bicarbonate of soda and salt and add to the sugar mixture, mixing well. Fold in bran flakes and sultanas. Drop rounded spoonfuls onto greased baking sheets. Bake at 190 °C (375 °F, gas 5) for 10–12 minutes. Cool on a wire rack, then store in a tightly covered container.

MAKES ABOUT 50 BISCUITS.

INDEX